T0108907

Carry This Message

CARRY THIS MESSAGE

A *Guide for Big Book Sponsorship*

JOE McQ.

August House, Inc.
ATLANTA

© 2002 by Joe McQ.
All rights reserved. This book, or parts thereof,
may not be reproduced without permission.
Published 2002 by August House, Inc.,

www.augusthouse.com.

Printed in the United States of America

10 9 8 7 6 5 4 3 2 1   HB

20 19 18 17 16 15 14   PB

LIBRARY OF CONGRESS CATALOGING-IN-PUBLICATION DATA

McQ, Joe, 1928–
    Carry this message : a guide for Big book sponsorship /
Joe McQ.
        p.   cm.
    Includes bibliographical references.
    ISBN 978-0-87483-653-0 (alk. paper)
    ISBN 978-0-87483-654-7 (pbk. : alk. paper)
    1. Alcoholics—Religious life. 2. W., Bill. Alcoholics
Anonymous. 3. Twelve-step programs—Religious
aspects—Christianity. I. Title.
BV4596.A48 .M354 2002
362.292'86—dc21
                                    2002018614

The excerpts from *Alcoholics Anonymous* and *Twelve Steps and Twelve Traditions* are reprinted with permission of Alcoholics Anonymous World Services, Inc. (A.A.W.S.). Permission to reprint these excerpts does not mean that A.A.W.S. has reviewed or approved the contents of this publication, or that A.A.W.S. necessarily agrees with the views expressed herein. A.A. is a program of recovery from alcoholism *only*—use of these excerpts in connection with programs and activities which are patterned after A.A., but which address other problems, or in any other non-A.A. context, does not imply otherwise.

AUGUST HOUSE, INC.   ATLANTA

For
Charlie C., Bob S., and Nan R.,
with gratitude.

Acknowledgments

The author and the editors are grateful to the following for their contributions to this book:

- Alcoholics Anonymous World Services, Inc., for permission to use the Steps and to quote from *Alcoholics Anonymous,* 3rd edition, and *Twelve Steps and Twelve Traditions;*
- The Board of the Kelly Foundation for its support of the project and for permission to use illustrations and adapt some text from *Recovery Dynamics;*
- Judith Faust, our wonderful editor of *Steps* and now of *Message;*
- Donna B. and Don B., Gayle Bailey, and Betty Sanders, supporters of our work in so many ways;
- All the folks at August House Publishers, particularly Ted and Liz Parkhurst;
- Lucille Chandler, Molly, Mitchell, and Loubelle, for all you give us.

Contents

A Note from the Editors

Several years after *The Steps We Took* was published, Joe began to talk with us about some changes he saw taking place. The treatment-center movement seemed to be waning, and for the first time, he said, membership in Alcoholics Anonymous was declining. Joe was particularly concerned that in our A.A. groups we had to some extent relinquished our responsibility, even our *ability*, to take new people through the first three Steps—that crucial work having been turned over for some years to the treatment centers. He believed that we needed to return to our responsibilities as recovering people to help new people through the *whole* program from beginning to end. This is when we first saw the need for *Carry This Message*.

Some things have not changed, notably the principles upon which A.A. was founded. In *Carry This Message*, as in *The Steps We Took*, Joe leads us back to the original text, *Alcoholics Anonymous*, for a review of the simple program that has brought joy and freedom to people in A.A., Al-Anon, and more than two hundred other organizations. And it's still true that alcoholism is a disease, that the only way to overcome the disease is a spiritual awakening, and that a thorough working of the Twelve Steps of Alcoholics Anonymous will bring about this spiritual awakening and bring us to sobriety and serenity. We learn in the Third Step Prayer on page 63 of the Big Book to ask our Higher Power to "take away our difficulties" so that our victory over our own difficulties will "bear witness" to those we would serve.

How we can serve most effectively is the focus of this book—how we can best pass on the principles of this simple program in meetings and in sponsorship. We believe that to achieve sobriety and serenity for ourselves, we must carry *this* message, the message found in the Big Book, to others. Joe McQuany, who taught the Steps all over the world for more than thirty years, offers here tried-and-true techniques for working with others, techniques simple to follow and true to the Big Book and the principles of our program. In these pages, Joe again shares his experience, strength, and hope and reminds us how A.A. meetings and sponsorship can best be used to reach our goal—a spiritual awakening.

It was a pleasure and privilege for us to work with Joe, to sit with him in the evenings, record his ideas, and put together this book—always striving to maintain the unique voice that was Joe's gift. We were truly blessed by our associations with this teacher whom the Higher Power used to carry *this* message to so many of us. We believe you will be blessed, too.

Huey C. and Sally C.
Little Rock, Arkansas

A note on the references: Unless otherwise specified, page numbers in the text refer to the Big Book, Alcoholics Anonymous.

The Twelve Steps of Alcoholics Anonymous

Here are the steps we took, which are suggested as a program of recovery:

1. We admitted we were powerless over alcohol—that our lives had become unmanageable.
2. Came to believe that a Power greater than ourselves could restore us to sanity.
3. Made a decision to turn our will and our lives over to the care of God *as we understood Him.*
4. Made a searching and fearless moral inventory of ourselves.
5. Admitted to God, to ourselves, and to another human being the exact nature of our wrongs.
6. Were entirely ready to have God remove all these defects of character.
7. Humbly asked Him to remove our shortcomings.
8. Made a list of all the people we had harmed, and became willing to make amends to them all.
9. Made direct amends to such people wherever possible, except when to do so would injure them or others.
10. Continued to take personal inventory and when we were wrong promptly admitted it.
11. Sought through prayer and meditation to improve our conscious contact with God *as we understood Him,* praying only for knowledge of His will for us and the power to carry that out.
12. Having had a spiritual awakening as the result of these Steps, we tried to carry this message to alcoholics, and to practice these principles in all our affairs.

Alcoholics Anonymous, 3d edition
New York: Alcoholics Anonymous World Services, Inc., 1976, pp. 59–60

Passing On a Special "Gift"

"Each group has but one primary purpose—to carry its message to the alcoholic who still suffers." Better to do one thing well than many badly. The life of our Fellowship depends on this principle. The ability of each A.A. to identify himself with and bring recovery to the newcomer is a gift from God . . . passing on this gift to others is our one aim. Sobriety can't be kept unless it is given away.

—Tradition Five, from *Twelve Steps and Twelve Traditions*

Once in a while we have to take a critical look at things, even the things we think are worthy and working well. Otherwise we may look up and find them gone.

Even A.A., as it has grown, has lost some of its message. We need to return to our message, to our roots.

Because of our tradition of anonymity, the only way the message can be carried is through the "Big Book," through meetings, and through sponsorship. There is no other way the suffering alcoholic is going to receive our message. The Big Book has never been changed, so it's authentic. But meetings have changed, and sponsorship has also changed and may have lost some of its effectiveness.

A.A. is not growing as fast as it once did, and there's a lot of conjecture as to why this is true. I think it might be because we have less A.A. in our meetings. The message is supposed to be delivered in meetings. I hear people say we need to carry the message to the treatment center, but I think we need to be sure to carry it to the meetings.

For the first twenty-five or thirty years, up until the

1960s, the message we heard in meetings was the same. There were about 150,000 people in the program. Groups still relied on the Big Book and the A.A. message. With the growth of the treatment center movement in the late sixties and early seventies, one of the biggest helps and one of the biggest hindrances to A.A. came along.

Although A.A. has no direct connection with treatment centers, they have certainly affected the program. Before the increase in the number of treatment centers, people who came to A.A. came from detox centers, or hospitals, or found us by word of mouth. A.A. members, through meetings and sponsorship, introduced the newcomer to the principles of the program, and he or she would be more or less "coerced" into working the Twelve Steps and in a timely way. You know, the alcoholic is put in a "box" by working Steps 1 and 2. Being in this box forces him or her to begin the program of recovery. Sponsorship is moving a person from one place to another; we do it Step by Step.

With the rise of treatment centers, newcomers began to come to us with what they had been exposed to there—lots of therapies: transactional analysis, reality therapy, and many others designed to treat *other problems.* Many people came to A.A. by way of treatment centers. These people came to A.A.—and continue to come to A.A.—with other philosophies and other ideas. And there has been a tendency for some of these ideas to dilute the A.A. message of recovery.

In the early days of A.A., sponsors would come to the alcoholic's home and talk him through Steps 1 and 2. Then they would come back, after they were thoroughly convinced he was ready, and start him on the program. The "first one hundred" people and people up through the 1960s became very skilled at working this beginning part of the program with people. But since the early seventies, when treatment centers came on the scene, alcoholics and addicts more typically have begun their recovery in treatment centers. When we saw the alcoholic in A.A., he or she had already been sober for thirty days, had already taken Steps 1 and 2. There wasn't as much pressure—there wasn't such a desperate need—to coerce him or her into thoroughly working the Steps. Often people got by with working the Steps in a more haphazard way. Some worked the program of action; some didn't.

So over the last twenty-five or thirty years, treatment centers have been supervising Steps 1 and 2 for us. Many sponsors in A.A. today have never had the experience of working the first Steps with a sponsoree! But now, with health care reforms and other social and political forces, the number of treatment centers is diminishing. There are fewer and fewer, and insurance companies are no longer as willing to pay for treatment as they were during the treatment-center boom. At the same time, we in A.A. have lost some of our skill in working with alcoholics in this important phase of their recovery.

Once again people are coming to get sober and find recovery in A.A. where few of us—few potential sponsors—have worked with wet drunks. We may even be offended when we smell alcohol on somebody's breath! But in the early days, newcomers were almost always still drinking when they made their initial approach to the program. I believe we need to reconsider our expectations and redevelop our skills for working with new members who come to us without having had the treatment center experience; that is part of my purpose in writing this book—to provide a guide to the whole of sponsorship, sponsorship based directly on the Big Book.

In the early days, nobody else was interested in working with drunks, but when the federal government became interested in the problem and started putting money into it, hospitals and other people became interested in it. At this point, in its policy of "cooperation without affiliation," A.A. allowed these entities to take over some of the work it had been doing. Often the first contact an A.A. member had with a new person was to take him to a treatment center. The A.A. member may never have said a word to the person about Steps 1 and 2. He just dropped him off at detox, and that was it. That was a typical Twelve Step call. We actually expected the treatment centers to prepare the person, and then when he came to us, we would give him the program.

So we have lost some of our skills. And now that the treatment centers may be closing down, we are faced with relearning something we used to be quite good at. People have all kinds of ideas about what's wrong with A.A.—it isn't spiritual enough and so forth—but I believe this is a big factor. An oldtimer told me that in the early days of A.A., maybe ninety-five percent of the people who showed up at meetings were drunk. They would have greeters at the door, often wives of the members, who greeted by sniffing. These "sniffers" would report to the oldtimers who was drinking and who wasn't. As you might guess, many of them were quite experienced sniffers!

Bill Wilson emphasized three pertinent ideas:

- that we were alcoholic and could not manage our own lives
- that probably no human power could have relieved our alcoholism
- that God could and would if He were sought (*Alcoholics Anonymous*, p. 60)

Without the "coercion" of being sold on these ideas, we have the phenomenon of people doing strange things like taking one Step a year, or one Step a month, and so forth— in other words, not really making use of Steps 1 and 2.

In the notion of taking steps, there is power. In this book, I have used words such as "dynamic" and "momentum" to describe the forward energy in the Steps. It's like a line of dominoes. Almost everyone has seen the force of energy move forward through an entire line of set-up dominoes, knocking every one down. The "domino effect" is applicable here. The first Step causes the second Step and so on. A person who takes each Step only on a schedule often loses this momentum and energy. It's no longer a process; it won't bring about a spiritual experience if done this way. The secret is the interaction of the Steps taken in sequence in a timely manner. If you are making a cake according to a recipe, you don't put the flour in this week, the eggs next week, and the milk a week later.

When I came to A.A., each home group had two meetings a week: a speaker meeting, at which a person would talk about his recovery, and a Twelve Step meeting. The purpose of the Twelve Step meeting was to make sure that new members could go through the Steps with the group's guidance. New people had the opportunity to get the program, and "old" people had the opportunity to work with the new people. Each person had a sponsor and was given so many weeks to work the Steps. Many of our meetings today have become "discussion" meetings, where people simply discuss their problems—like group therapy.

Tradition Five says, "Each group has but one primary purpose—to carry its message to the alcoholic who still suffers." If we refocused on the Big Book, on the Twelve Steps, on our message, I think we would see a lot more recovery. In the foreword to the second edition of the Big Book, it was estimated that 75 percent of the people who began the program, who began taking the Steps, got sober: "Of alcoholics who came to A.A. and really tried, 50% got sober at once and remained that way; 25% sobered up after some relapses . . ." (p. xx). But today fewer than five percent of people who go to their first A.A. meeting get sober.

The fellowship we have today grew out of the Big Book, *Alcoholics Anonymous,* written by "the first 100" people. But the fellowship has grown so big that I'm afraid many groups are not using the Big Book as they once did. I think members of every group ought to ask themselves, "Are we really carrying the message of Alcoholics Anonymous?"

What we need to say in our meetings is, "The things that you learned in the treatment centers may be helpful to you, but this is A.A. Here is our message."

Think about it: if you only have an hour for a meeting, every bit of the time that you use for other things, other subjects, pushes out the Steps. I've been to groups where after they read the Preamble, you didn't hear another word about A.A.

If you think of the "first 100," of Bill Wilson and Dr. Bob Smith and the sacrifices they made, you realize they were heroes. And people today who work to bring the fellowship back on course, they are heroes, too.

Often an entire meeting will center around people discussing their problems, yet at no time during that meeting will anyone tell those people what our program says to do about their problems. We have a Step that answers any problem we have. And people who have had the spiritual experience that results from working these Steps *want* to share their experience. They know what they did, and they can help others by carrying this message. Indeed, we are compelled by Step 12 to "carry this message."

We're fighting a tide of other information and other approaches. Basically the only A.A. plan is the Big Book plan. If you understand the plan in the Big Book, you realize that it's simple and that nothing is more effective.

In the last ten or fifteen years, there's been a trend back toward learning about the Big Book. Most communities have Big Book Study groups. I'm in a Big Book Study, and my guess is at least half the people who show up end up getting sober. I've seen lots of young women there lately—more drug addicts than alcoholics, from rough, seemingly hopeless situations. I've seen them pull themselves together and become happy, productive people. They hold jobs, and they help other people. The program in the Big Book is still changing lives.

I'm afraid we're losing some oldtimers, too. The oldtimers' growth comes through helping newcomers to work the Steps. If carrying this message is not going on in the group, oldtimers may lose interest in the fellowship.

We all love Alcoholics Anonymous. It saved our lives. But somewhere along the way, without our realizing it, some of the principles have gotten lost. When we start losing the message, we start losing the fellowship.

Step 12 says, "Having had a spiritual awakening as the result of these steps, we tried to carry this message to alcoholics, and to practice these principles in all our affairs." So the key is to keep asking ourselves, "What is *this message?*" And there should be no controversy about what this message is. "Having had a spiritual awakening as the result of these steps . . ."—this is the message we are to carry.

If we work these Steps, we will have a spiritual awakening. It should be obvious that in order to carry this message, you must have worked the Steps yourself and had a spiritual awakening as a result. In the Preamble to our Wednesday night Big Book Study, we say, "If you have taken these Steps and have gotten results, please share your experience. If you have not taken these Steps, please be willing to listen."

Beyond our meetings, we carry this message through sponsorship of others. Chapter Seven in the Big Book, "Working With Others," is devoted entirely to carrying this message. It tells you what to do and when to do it. It also tells you what not to do.

> Dr. Carl Jung told Rowland Hazard, "I believe that every human being has an inner search for wholeness. I have never been able to help a person who found their wholeness in alcohol. It requires a power greater than human power." I think God created us with that emptiness so we would find it has to be filled by spirituality.

Nowadays sponsorship has become more friendship than it was in the early days. A lot of the emphasis is on socializing; people go out for coffee with new members after meetings. This is fine, but it is not the primary relationship the sponsor needs with his sponsoree. If a friendship comes first, sponsors may not feel as free to say things that need to be said. At first, anyway, a relationship of mutual respect is better. After a while, friendship may develop, but it could make sponsorship more difficult in the beginning of the relationship. We need to spend our time helping people work the Steps. We need to be more aware of what A.A. is and what it is not.

I think some people quit drinking, work some of the Steps, and start sponsoring. But if you haven't had a spiritual awakening, you can't carry "this message" to other people. The Big Book says, "You cannot transmit something you haven't got" (p. 164).

So the first qualification for sponsorship is to have

worked the Steps yourself, and to have had your own spiritual awakening.

We say this is a program of attraction. New people aren't going to be attracted to people who are simply not drinking. Not drinking is not enough. We often place the emphasis on sobriety, but that isn't the goal of this program. The goal of this program is a spiritual awakening that will change our lives, that will produce a personality change sufficient to make us recover, to make us happy, joyous, and free. If people can see that has happened to us—in us—they will be attracted to our program. This is our message.

Unfortunately, there are some miserable people attending A.A. These people are just not drinking. The Big Book tells us that the tools of our program will enable us to enter a "fourth dimension," to live better lives than most other people on earth. But too often we settle for not drinking.

If we are to carry this message, we need to be reminded what a powerful message it is. "Having had a spiritual awakening as the result of these steps . . ."—this is the message we carry to others.

The existence of the fellowship depends on it. Lives depend on it.

The best advice comes from Chapter 7 of the Big Book:

- Find out all you can about the prospect.
- Don't deal with him when he is drunk.
- Never force yourself on him.
- Place this book where he can see it.
- See him alone (without his family).

———

- Tell him enough about your own drinking to encourage him to speak of himself.
- Do not yet tell him what you did to recover.
- Describe yourself as an alcoholic.
- Tell him about your struggles to stop.
- Show him the mental twists which lead to the first drink.

———

- Be careful not to brand him as an alcoholic.
- If he thinks he can still control his drinking, tell him that that is possible if he is not too alcoholic, but if he is, there is little chance he can recover on his own.
- Speak of alcoholism as an illness.
- Tell him about the conditions of the mind and the body that characterize the disease.
- Let him ask you how you got well.

———

- Tell him exactly what happened to you.
- Make it clear that he does not have to agree with your concept of God.

- Let him see that you are not there to instruct him in religion.
- Outline the program of action.
- Make it clear that he is under no obligation to see you again if he doesn't want to.

- Do not contradict his defensive views.
- Tell him about the fellowship and offer to lend him your book.
- Give him a chance to think it over.
- Do not crusade.
- Do not talk down to him.

- Show him how the steps worked for you.
- Offer him friendship and fellowship.
- Tell him if he wants to get well, you will do anything to help.
- If he only wants you to be a banker or nurse, you may drop him.
- If he wants to see you again, ask him to read the Big Book in the interval.

- If he thinks he can do the job some other way, encourage him to follow his own conscience.
- If he asks for a second visit, has read the Book, and is ready to go through the Twelve Steps, offer to give him practical advice.
- Even if he doesn't want the Program, you may offer it to his family.

- Make sure he understands that he can recover in spite of anyone.
- Do not participate in his family quarrels.
- Never show intolerance or hatred of drinking as an institution.

A Synchronicity of Events

The A.A. society traces its beginnings to a May 1935 meeting of two men in Akron, Ohio . . .

—Mel B., *New Wine*

To work successfully with others, it's helpful to know the "chain of events," as Bill Wilson put it, that brought the "first forty" people together to write the Steps, to write *Alcoholics Anonymous,* and to launch the fellowship of the same name.

Many people in Alcoholics Anonymous and other Twelve-Step groups know the names of Bill and Lois Wilson and Dr. Bob and Anne Smith and their roles in founding A.A. and Al-Anon. A miraculous synchronicity of events led to the powerful dynamics of recovery followed in A.A. and many other Twelve-Step groups.

Let's begin in Switzerland in 1931, where Rowland Hazard, a New York investment banker suffering from alcoholism, sought help from the great psychologist Dr. Carl Jung. Dr. Jung told Rowland there might be hope he could stay sober—if he could have a personality change through a spiritual experience.

Rowland returned to New York and found an Oxford Group, where he sought a spiritual experience. The Oxford Groups were informal fellowships of people from any and all religions who were not satisfied with their spiritual progress. Anyone could join and work through the tenets of the Group to get some spiritual growth and change their lives. The groups weren't particularly focused on the problem of alcoholism.

Frank Buchman, a Lutheran minister, was the originator of the Oxford Groups. As a young man he had directed a boys' school in Philadelphia where he came to have an argument with his board members. He got mad, resigned, and left the country to travel in Europe. In England in 1908, he went to a church meeting one night and heard a woman, Jessie Penn-Lewis, preach on resentments and forgiveness. And he was greatly moved by what he heard.

Realizing that he held a resentment against the six board members in Philadelphia who had offended him, Buchman went back to his room that night, sat down, and wrote them a letter asking for their forgiveness. He later said that this action produced a sudden change in his life. An instant change.

He never heard back from these people, but he began to reflect on how his life was tremendously improved. He began to ask himself, *How did that happen? What did I do to bring that about? If I can understand what I did, I can renew myself in any way I want to. Better than that, I can show someone else how to do it.*

As he sought to understand his experience, Buchman listed the things he had done: (1) he had surrendered, (2) he had examined his sins, (3) he had shared and confessed, (4) he had made restitution, and (5) he had asked for God's guidance. So he began telling other people how to do this. He said that when we do these simple things, then, and only then, can we receive God's guidance.

Buchman was immediately successful. People who followed this procedure were changed. The Oxford Groups grew and spread. Realizing that these five basic principles—these tenets—were the foundation of Christianity (and of other religions worldwide), Buchman called his movement "First-Century Christian Fellowship."

So when Rowland Hazard returned to New York after consulting Dr. Jung in Switzerland, he joined an Oxford Group and started using its tenets. Doing so produced in him the change and the spiritual experience he sought—and as a result he stayed sober until he died.

As he found sobriety, Rowland heard that an old friend, Ebby Thatcher, was about to be committed to a mental institution for his alcoholism. Rowland took a couple of his Oxford Group friends to the court, and the judge turned Ebby over to them. Rowland took Ebby to his home, and in two weeks worked with him through the Oxford Group's tenets. Then he took Ebby to the Reverend Sam Shoemaker's Calvary Mission in New York City, where he worked with people suffering with alcoholism. Ebby's work at the mission with the alcoholics became an important part of his recovery.

One day Ebby thought about his longtime friend Bill Wilson, and he wondered whether Bill might be interested in what he was doing to get sober. This was November 1934. Bill Wilson had been to Towns Hospital in 1933 for his alcoholism and again in the summer of 1934, and Dr. William Silkworth[1] there had told him the problem: that alcoholism was a hopeless allergy and obsession.

Bill Wilson had gained an understanding of the problem from Dr. Silkworth, but he didn't have a solution until Ebby walked into his kitchen in 1934, shared with him what they had found about the solution, and laid out the program of action for recovery.

Bill would have to make one more hospital stay for his illness. In *Alcoholics Anonymous Comes of Age,* Bill described

---

[1]Dr. Silkworth had become interested in alcoholics as an intern at Bellview Hospital. Most doctors don't like to work with alcoholics because they don't usually have much success with them. But Dr. Silkworth had spent a lot of time with them. When the stock market crashed in 1929, he lost his private practice and found himself at Towns Hospital working with alcoholics again. He worked with alcoholics the rest of his life, treating more than 50,000.

admitting his "bottom" and having a dramatic spiritual experience:

> My depression deepened unbearably and finally it seemed to me as though I were at the very bottom of the pit . . . finally, just for the moment, the last vestige of my proud obstinacy was crushed. All at once I found myself crying out, "If there is a God, let Him show Himself! I am ready to do anything, anything!" Suddenly the room lit up with a great white light . . . It burst upon me that I was a free man . . . All about me and through me there was a wonderful feeling of Presence. (p. 63)

Ebby visited Bill at Towns Hospital. When Bill asked him, he again provided the Oxford Group's program, through which Ebby had found his own sobriety.

Dr. Silkworth had observed that when Bill worked with other alcoholics, he didn't drink. So when Bill Wilson left the hospital, Dr. Silkworth suggested to him that he continue to find other alcoholics to work with.

And Bill did work with others, trying to get them to "surrender," the first step of the Oxford Groups. He told drunks that they needed to "find God." He was trying to help them, but most alcoholics looked at him like, *What's wrong with this guy? Is he some kind of fanatic or something?*

He hadn't helped anyone. One day he went back to Towns Hospital; Dr. Silkworth thought there was value in letting Bill talk to the patients. Bill told him, "I've been trying to help alcoholics for six months and nobody will listen."

Dr. Silkworth said something like, "Bill, I think you are going about it all wrong. You're trying to get those people to have a great-white-flash type of spiritual experience like you had. I think you ought to first tell them what I told you about the allergy and obsession, the problem. Then they may see the hopelessness of what they are doing, and they may try your program."

The very next alcoholic Bill talked with was Dr. Bob Smith. Bill had traveled to Akron, Ohio, in a proxy fight involving a small company there. His side lost the battle; his business acquaintances were discouraged and left him there in the Mayflower Hotel with only ten dollars in his pocket. He felt that he was about to drink. At home in New York when he had this feeling, he'd go find an alcoholic to talk to. Helping other alcoholics helped him. So he did the same thing in Akron.

Dr. Bob Smith was a member of the Oxford Group in Akron. He had confided in the group, "This may cost me my profession, but I can't stop drinking." The other six members must surely have offered to pray for him.

The story goes that the Akron Oxford Group wrote down the guidance they received in their morning meditations. They felt God would give them insights in this way into what they should do. One day Henrietta Seiberling, a member of the Oxford Group in Akron of which Dr. Bob was a part, wrote down from her morning meditation God's guidance that "Dr. Bob should not drink one more drop of whiskey."

Soon—a few weeks later—Bill Wilson came to Akron. He got the names of local ministers from the church directory in the hotel. He called Rev. Walter Tunks, who as it happened was involved with the Oxford Groups. Rev. Tunks told him, "I'm busy but I can get you in touch with somebody who can get you in touch with somebody." And he gave Bill Henrietta's name.

Although Dr. Bob had been in the Oxford Groups for two years, he was still drinking. He knew the solution; he knew the program of action. But before Bill found him, he thought of his drinking as a "sin." Minding his own sobriety, Bill sat down with him and explained the problem, as Dr. Silkworth had to him, as an allergy and obsession. Amazingly, a stockbroker told a doctor the "exact nature of the problem."

Once Dr. Bob saw the problem in this way, he started to recover. Not only did Bill help Dr. Bob, but also he learned the effectiveness of carrying the message in this way. Bill and Dr. Bob went to the hospital together to visit a man named Bill Dodson. Together they told him about the problem, the solution, and the program of action; he took it and recovered. That's when A.A. as we know it today began.

Soon the action principles began to fall into line. This became the program of the "first one hundred."

Since 1935, the fellowship of Alcoholics Anonymous has expressed an advanced spiritual approach to solving human problems . . .

—Mel B., *New Wine*

After visiting with the Oxford Group members in Akron, Bill went back to New York with a better understanding of their program. And he went back with knowledge of the powerful dynamics he had learned in Akron: the problem, the solution, and the program of action.

So Bill Wilson was the first person to have the whole program of recovery. He had gotten

the *problem* from Dr. Silkworth,

the *solution* from Ebby, who had gotten it from Rowland, who had gotten it from Dr. Jung, and

the *program of action* from the Oxford Groups.

Thus the Twelve Steps have their origins in the ideas of Dr. William Silkworth, Dr. Carl Jung, and the Oxford Groups. Bill Wilson always emphasized that he had nothing to do with originating any of these ideas; his contribution was to gather them together from other people. He always felt he was used as an instrument to put together the Twelve Steps.

The Program of Recovery

THE PROBLEM
    Step 1
    1930
    Dr. Silkworth

THE SOLUTION
    Step 2
    1931
    Dr. Jung

PROGRAM OF ACTION
    Steps 3–12
    Oxford Group tenets

Bill expanded the Oxford Group's tenets, and this is what he, Dr. Bob Smith, and the "first one hundred" got sober on. Although they got sober in the Oxford Groups, Bill felt that alcoholics needed to change more drastically than other members of the Oxford Groups did. He realized the tenets needed to be adapted and the meetings made separate for alcoholics.

When he wrote the Steps in 1938, Bill Wilson did a lot more than just put them together. He found language alcoholics were more likely to respond to. Bill knew he couldn't accept—and he didn't believe most alcoholics could accept— traditional religious terms like "surrender," "witness," and "sin."

The first Oxford Group tenet was "surrender." Bill

replaced the word "surrender," which he didn't think most self-centered alcoholics could tolerate, with "[m]ade a decision to turn our will and our lives over to the care of God as we understood Him." It's the same idea, but with less religious-sounding language.

The second Oxford Group Step was "examine your sins." Bill changed that to "[m]ade a searching and fearless moral inventory . . ." The Oxford Groups' "sharing and confessing" became "admitted to God, to ourselves, and to another human being the exact nature of our wrongs."

Bill added Steps 6 and 7. Then he added Step 10. Steps 6, 7, and 10 were included as tools for change; Bill thought the Steps needed to provide for more change since alcoholics needed more change. He divided "making restitution" into Steps 8 and 9. The last Oxford Group tenet was "asked God for guidance." Bill didn't think alcoholics would like that much, so he changed it to Step 11: "Sought through prayer and meditation to improve our conscious contact with God as we understood Him."

Bill didn't like the word "witness" as the Oxford Groups used it either. He had been in the Oxford Groups for four years by this time, and every drunk he tried to work with had a helluva problem with this language. But as he, Ebby, and Dr. Bob had certainly learned, it was an important part of recovery. Bill phrased this necessary Step, "Having had a spiritual awakening as the result of these steps, we tried to carry this message to other alcoholics."

OXFORD GROUP TENETS	A.A.'S STEPS 3, 4, 5, 8, 9, 11, AND 12
Surrendering	Made a conscious decision to turn our will and our lives over to the care of God as we understood Him.
Examining sins	Made a searching and fearless moral inventory of ourselves.
Sharing and confessing	Admitted to God, to ourselves, and to another human being the exact nature of our wrongs.
Making restitution	Made a list of all the persons we had harmed, and became willing to make amends to them all. Made direct amends to such people wherever possible, except when to do so would injure them or others.
Asking God for guidance	Sought through prayer and meditation to improve our conscious contact with God as we understood Him.
Witnessing	Having had a spiritual awakening as the result of these steps, we tried to carry this message to alcoholics and to practice these principles in all our affairs.

Bill Wilson adapted
the tenets and added
Steps 1, 2, 6, 7, and 10.

Carrying This Message to Others

You can help when no one else can.

You can secure their confidence when others fail . . .

To watch people recover, to see them help others,
to watch loneliness vanish, to see a fellowship
grow up about you, to have a host of friends—
this is an experience you will not want to miss.

—Bill W.,
Alcoholics Anonymous

The word *sponsorship* is not in the Big Book. There is not an official way to sponsor, but we have enough history, enough experience, to know what works. There are people who pick up others and take them to meetings and say they are sponsoring them. This can be helpful, but it's not really sponsoring. Many of the nice things we do can be positive, but not if they crowd out true sponsorship.

What is sponsorship then? Sponsorship is guiding someone through the Steps—through the problem, the solution, and the program of action—to recovery.

In the early days, members would go to a sponsoree's home and visit with him to see that he understood Step 1. Then they would come back in a few days and see whether the person believed in God. If the prospect agreed that he was powerless over alcohol, and that he believed in God, his sponsor would accompany him to the Oxford Group. He would tell the members of the group, "This man is an alcoholic. He says that he believes in God. I would like to sponsor him in this group." They'd start him on what is now Step 3. Two or three members would go upstairs in Dr. Bob's house with the person, get down on their knees and help him take Step 3. Alcoholics couldn't join the Oxford Group until they were qualified through taking Steps 1 and 2.

Nowadays people who are attempting to sponsor a new person often say, "Go read 'How it Works.'" The problem is the person hasn't had a chance to really get the essential principles that come from the information and insights in Steps 1 and 2, the problem and the solution, unless he has read the first four chapters that explain the problem and the solution.

The chapter in the Big Book called "Working With Others" says to try to find out something about the person by talking to her family, but in many cases that can't be done. You might just meet somebody at a meeting or somebody might ask you about being her sponsor. There is a difference now in the way we go about getting together with people to sponsor.

"Working With Others" was written many years ago, long before we had the many treatment centers and detox centers we now have. We don't often bring someone to our homes for their first approach to sobriety as Bill recommends in that chapter. Now we often take them to a treatment center.

Another difference between the early days and now is working with the families. Bill suggests that the sponsor spend some time helping the alcoholic's family understand what's happening. The sponsor had to work with the family in those days as best he could. But now we have almost as many Al-Anon groups (including Alateen and Adult Children of Alcoholics) as A.A. groups, and most of us refer the family members to these groups where they learn to work the same Steps as the alcoholic.

At the time the Big Book was written, masculine terms and pronouns ("man," "men," "he," "him," and so on) were generally used, even to include both genders. In some contexts "man," for instance, meant a human being. Bill also saw most alcoholics as men, but now there are probably as many women getting sober through the principles of the Twelve Steps as there are men. (And, of course, using "man" or "men" meaning both genders isn't as acceptable.)

Nowadays, too, we are working with younger people, people who have often not sunk to the depths of alcoholism that we did formerly. Still our major responsibility as sponsors is to guide the person through the Steps, passing on the message of recovery.

In the early going, the sponsor should find out about the person through conversation. Some people say that they work the same way with every sponsoree, but I don't think you can really do that. It's true we all have some important things in common—our inability to drink normally, for instance—but everybody is different in other ways. I think we should work with each person in the way that best suits him or her.

At the same time, some guidelines do have to be established because we are working with an undisciplined person. Assignments should be given, and the sponsor should make it clear to the person that assignments have to be done by a specific time. In my experience, this is the best way to work with an alcoholic.

As sponsors, we know there are certain things we require of a sponsoree: he has to be willing to go to any lengths to get sober, and if he expects you to work with him, he has to carry out his assignments and do the things you ask him to do.

It is also important to work the Steps in sequence and not to draw the work out over too long a time. I have heard of people taking a week or even a month on each Step. That is *not* an effective approach. The process works better when we work one Step and then immediately work the next. Keep your sponsoree moving!

Dr. Bob once walked into a hospital and asked a man, "Young man, do you believe you are an alcoholic?"

"Yes, sir," he answered.

"Do you believe in God?"

"Yes, sir."

Dr. Bob said, "Get down on your knees." And they took Step 3. That amounted to doing the first three Steps in less than a minute!

Many people don't understand about working with alcoholics. They may say, "Well, alcoholics are so new and unaccustomed to the way we do things that I don't think you can get them to do it." But an alcoholic can do just about anything you make her do. If you insist that she do certain things, she'll get them done. She has to go from undisciplined to very disciplined, and the sponsor is the one who helps her build the bridge between the two.

"We alcoholics are undisciplined, so we let God discipline us in the simple way we have just outlined."

—*Alcoholics Anonymous,* p. 88

At our treatment center, Serenity Park, we require that all the clients get a sponsor in their third week. The sponsor teaches discipline; the program teaches discipline; everything is working on this undisciplined person. An undisciplined person may fight discipline, but it has to be enforced to help the person. If he had had that discipline, he wouldn't be in the shape he's in.

Bill Wilson reminds us in the Big Book that suffering alcoholics are very sick people. We are dealing with very sick, undisciplined people. We have to take this into consideration sometimes when they *don't* do everything we ask them to do. Sometimes sponsors forget this and try to demand too much of their sponsorees, but these undisciplined people are going to make some mistakes.

I believe the sponsor should take Step 5 with the sponsoree whether he or she is in a treatment center or wherever. When a sponsor looks at a person's Step 4, it will be obvious whether he has taken the first three Steps. If he hasn't done the first three Steps, it will be impossible for him to have done a thorough inventory. A sponsor has to be involved at this point to learn something about the person and work with him or her into recovery.

Some treatment centers have the clients do Steps 1, 2, and 3. Some ask them to do 1 through 4. But the Twelve Steps were designed to be taken in sequence and with a certain rhythm or momentum; it shouldn't take more than thirty days to work them all. At Serenity Park, we do all the action Steps through Step 9, and the last three are for Aftercare.

I didn't choose my own sponsor; he chose me. He always told me that he and some other guys drew straws and he lost! Some people like to only sponsor one person at a time. When you sponsor a person, you need to commit yourself to spending some time with that person. Some people have ten or twenty sponsorees, but I don't see how they can pay enough attention to that many people to be really helpful. That's often ego on the sponsor's part. And, you know, when you sponsor so many, you are also depriving another alcoholic of the opportunity to sponsor someone. Sometimes people who live out of town will ask me to sponsor them, but I always advise them to get someone in their own group, someone who can spend more time with them.

I've found one of my best A.A. rules is this: whatever I don't really want to do is the exact thing I need to do. Sometimes this means if there is somebody you really don't want to sponsor, he or she might be just the person you need to sponsor. We often get a first impression that's wrong. We may not like someone at first. We may not want to give the person a chance. But often the person we read that way is someone who can really add something to our own recovery. Alcoholics aren't always loving at first, you know. Alcoholism isn't a loving disease.

We often are drawn to people we recognize as being a lot like ourselves, but when we get out of our comfort zone, we can usually grow more. We have this in common: we are all alcoholics. This is enough.

We need to qualify our sponsorees by their willingness to do what we ask of them. Is the sponsoree *willing* to be sponsored? Is the sponsor *capable* of sponsoring? (That is, has he or she worked the Steps and had a spiritual awakening?) These are the only qualifications for either role. We are all qualified by "a desire to stop drinking." It's why we're all here.

What kind of relationship will you have with the person you're sponsoring? How will you establish it? People sometimes tell stories about how mean or how harsh their sponsor is. It shouldn't be that kind of relationship. There is firmness involved, and there must be respect, but it is *a kind and loving relationship*—one that's probably going to last for years. It needs to be skillfully forged.

Sometimes we don't really know how to sponsor. I hope this book will be helpful for you in sponsoring others. But the truth is it's pretty simple: a sponsor guides the sponsoree through the problem, the solution, and the program of action to a point of recovery. When the sponsoree gets there, he or she can guide somebody else through.

HOW SHOULD *THE NEW PERSON* GO ABOUT CHOOSING A SPONSOR?

Someone seeking a sponsor can qualify a prospective sponsor by asking whether he or she has worked the Steps.

There aren't any infallible rules for this, but here are some guidelines: the sponsoree shouldn't insist on getting somebody his or her exact age; he or she shouldn't necessarily choose somebody who does the same type of work. I've seen priests successfully sponsored by truck drivers. The sponsoree shouldn't go by the length of the prospective sponsor's sobriety. Some people who think they have to have a person with years and years of sobriety are just building their egos. In choosing a sponsor, the person should go by the *quality of sobriety* rather than its length.

The new person has to keep an open mind. He or she can listen to a person's comments in meetings, and if he or she is convinced the person has worked the Steps, that person will probably be a good choice for a sponsor.

ASSIGNMENT FOR STEP 1

READING . . . FOR SPONSOREE

Ask the sponsoree to read "The Doctor's Opinion" (p. xxiii) and "Bill's Story" (p. 1), both in the Big Book.

Have the sponsoree write a summary of each one. The summary should show an understanding of the problem. In alcoholism, the problem is a physical allergy and a mental obsession that make the alcoholic unable to drink normally.

DISCUSSION . . . FOR SPONSOR

Go over the assignment with your sponsoree, emphasizing the information about the physical craving and its causes in the body, and about the mental obsession. Make sure the sponsoree understands the problem.

Understanding the Problem

Quicksand stretched around me in all directions.
I had met my match. Alcohol was my master.
—Bill W.,
Alcoholics Anonymous

STEP 1:
We admitted we were powerless over
alcohol—that our lives had become
unmanageable.

Step 1 names the problem. The importance of Step 1—
of knowing the problem—cannot be overemphasized.
Remember that Dr. Bob Smith had been in the Oxford
Group for two years, and he had the solution, a spiritual
experience, and the program of action, the Oxford Group
tenets; but until Bill Wilson brought him *an understanding
of the problem,* he was unable to get sober. With knowledge
of the problem, which Dr. Silkworth had given Bill, Dr. Bob
had all the pieces—the problem, the solution, and the program of action. You first have to be sure the person you're
working with understands the problem.

All of us have come to this program as a result of the
constant frustration and constant defeat and pain we experienced drinking or using. We came to a willingness to take
Step 1. The pain brings on this willingness:

Under the lash of alcoholism, we are driven to A.A., and there we discover the fatal nature of our situation. Then, and only then, do we become as open-minded to conviction and as willing to listen as the dying can be. We stand ready to do anything which will lift the merciless obsession from us. (*Twelve Steps and Twelve Traditions,* p. 24)

Step 1 is hard to help someone else with. The person has to arrive at the point of unbearable pain and frustration alone. Some people can take more pain than others.

A person must become willing to change. Willingness is a state of mind that will allow a person to believe, to decide, and to act. We can understand what Bill Wilson meant when he said that Step 1 is the foundation of the principles. The second Step is believing, the third Step is deciding, and Steps 4 through 11 are action. They are all based on the foundation of willingness to change. Willingness to change comes about from no longer accepting the situation that you are in. That's what promotes change. It has to be totally and one hundred percent *not* accepting the situation that you are in. Once you do that, you can make a change.

So willingness is the key. It makes no difference what the problem is. To be willing to change, we have to realize that where we are at this time is never going to work—and that it's a waste of energy trying to make it work. Then we will be open to other possibilities. It doesn't matter whether the problem is alcohol, drugs, food, other people—this is why we have more than two hundred other groups using the Steps that were originally designed to show people how to recover from alcoholism. In fact, far more people are using the Twelve Steps to solve problems than are working with professionals, simply because the principles can be applied to any problem.

But, you know, as long as you think you can solve a problem on your own, you are not looking for any change. Sometimes I have something that needs fixing and I don't know much about it. I may try to put something together; when it won't work, I try it again, but it still won't work. Somebody watching me might say, "I don't think it's going to work that way. You ought to try . . ." But I say, "Get out of my way; I know what I'm doing." I can just keep on trying to force it, beating on it with a hammer or whatever.

Finally I realize a hundred percent that it's *not* going to work that way. I can't turn it around—I can't try a new way—until I give up on my way. This willingness is tough to come by because we have to give up on our way. Throughout our lives we're willing to give up on older gadgets and keep trying newer and better ones, but we're really stubborn about giving up running our lives by our own will. This willingness to change does not come easy for us.

In Step 1 we don't really know what we are going to do next. We just have to say, "What I'm doing is not working. I give up." But when we give up on our old ways, all kinds of possibilities open up for us! When we surrender our will, we become open to new and wonderful ways of seeing the world and of dealing with it.

We have to give up the old ways. We have to surrender. Surrender is important throughout all the Steps. It is the principle in changing directions. In order to change directions, we have to change our will.

Self-will gives us tunnel vision. When we are depending on self-will, we assume we can make progress, we assume we know it all. But we don't know it all. When we are trying to live by self-will, it's like trying to put something together the wrong way; it's living our lives based on a lie. So the idea is to surrender. When we surrender our will, all kinds of possibilities open for us. If we can give up on self-will, we can gain a broader view of things, of God's will and the will of others.

You can't force anybody to do this. But the power of this willingness to change is boundless; you can keep this willingness all your life, allow these principles to work, and your life will keep getting better and better. A lot of us find it easy to become complacent after we have gotten sober and reached a certain comfort zone. But if we continue to apply these principles of willingness and surrender in our lives, we can continue to become better and better.

The whole scheme of recovery is to be able to become sober and to continue to change your life. In the entire sixty years of this very human movement, the greatest failures have been the distortion of the principles by we who use them. We've lost a lot of the effectiveness of the program because people come into the fellowship and don't drink but *don't try to make changes in their lives.* I've heard it said that fewer than half the people in A.A. actually take all the Steps! But in the beginning, all the people in the program took the Steps; they used the principles. The Steps—and the Big Book—were originally written to show people how to make changes and improve their whole lives.

The sponsoree has to take Step 1 by himself. Booze makes him take it. It's a total collapse: he has to say, "I give up. I can't take it anymore." After he does that, a sponsor can work with him.

After the sponsoree takes this Step, she will become open to a new way. When she is still able to do it her way, she can't and won't be open to other possibilities.

I remember the day my own recovery started. An hour before, I wasn't thinking anything about it. Then all at once, I had a realization of total defeat. Bill talks about his realization in the Big Book when he says, "Quicksand stretched around me in all directions. I had met my match. Alcohol was my master" (p. 8). It had been his master for many years, but he had not been able to see it until that moment. For me, it was about 10:30 in the morning and I was sitting in a bar, doing my usual thing. I had been drunk for six weeks. All at once the idea came to me, "You can't go on this way. This is *never* going to work." I was convinced one hundred percent: what I had been doing was never going to work.

The next thing that came to my mind was that I needed some kind of help. I hadn't needed any help until that moment. Most alcoholics in the grip of their illness are not aware of the reality that they need help. But another alcoholic can give information about his problem, tell what he has done, and bring them closer to reality.

In those days, all we had for treatment was commitment to the state hospital, so I went and committed myself. The law said you could be committed, or you could commit yourself. Still, there wasn't any true alcohol treatment; the staff didn't know anything about alcoholism. They just put you in there and gave you some Thorazine. Four days later, I went to my first meeting on the ward.

I know now how fortunate I was—because everything seemed to be done right. This guy walked in there and talked about *his* problems. That's what you do first. He didn't say *anything* about me. He talked in great depth about the problems he had had. His problems seemed to me much more severe than the problems I was having, and my problem was overwhelming. I saw my problem through his problem; I found myself in his story.

After the meeting, I went over and asked him, "What do you think I should do?" (That's what the Big Book says: "Let him ask you.")

He looked at me and said, "Fellow, I was telling you what I did. Frankly, I don't give a damn what you do. Your problem is yours, and my problem is mine. But if you want me to show you what I did, I will show you." That's the way we got started. He showed me what he had done.

As a sponsor, the first thing you can do to help another alcoholic is tell him or her about your problem. That's the only thing the conversation is going to be about. When you meet, tell her about your problem. She is going to be very defensive because she thinks you are going to do like everybody else and tell her about *her* problem. She'll find herself in your story if she has the problem.

The twelfth Step doesn't say "carry *the* message." It says "carry *this* message." The message we carry is this: we have had a spiritual awakening as a result of these Steps. Our message is not just some conversation. A suffering alcoholic is not going to listen to anything that doesn't have depth and weight. You have to tell your story; it has to have happened to you. With the right information and the right kind of help, you can be successful in getting people to the point of willingness.

The information that alcoholism is a disease, an allergy, and an obsession got Dr. Bob to that point. He already knew the solution and the program of recovery, but he was still drunk. It wasn't until Bill brought him that piece of information that the principles were complete, and he was able to start becoming sober.

When we realize that what we have been doing is never going to work, we shut the door to the old. We come to a state of willingness. Suddenly all other possibilities open up for us.

The sponsoree has taken all of his or her energy for the last few years and devoted it to how to drink. It takes a lot of energy and a lot of lying to find the answer to "How can I drink?" (Things like "I don't have a drinking problem if I only drink beer. So I'll only drink beer.") When we shut the door on "How can I drink?," we take on an *easier* problem: "How can I stay sober?"

When we believe we can stay sober, we give the mind the challenge of finding that way. But first we have to shut off the old ideas. Because while we are still trying to find a way to drink successfully, we are constantly coming up with ideas, thinking, "Well, maybe I can make it work this new way." We have to start by getting our mind out of that. So willingness comes from a higher power: sometimes from another person, sometimes from getting some more information.

I think the willingness to change is a gift from God. It's a realization. We can't arrive there by ourselves; we can't see it entirely on our own. It's a window that opens up and gives us a flash of the truth—and we become willing to change.

As I think back on my situation that morning, I recall I had been in a lot more difficult situations than I was in that particular morning. I had been worse off. I don't think it just comes through pain. I've seen people come into the program who didn't seem to be in real bad situations, and I've seen people keep drinking to the point of death.

It's complex. The realization probably comes from different places. When Bill called Rev. Tunks that night in Akron, Rev. Tunks told him he was too busy to help him right then, but he gave him Henrietta's phone number. She and her Oxford Group had been praying for Dr. Bob. And here came Bill with an understanding of the problem, all that Dr. Bob needed to start getting well! That's the way it works sometimes: somebody shows up when you're in need. You just have to be willing to listen.

Everybody's first encounter with a sober alcoholic may be like mine was. The man who said to me, "I don't give a damn what *you* do," was short with me, but he woke me up. Everybody who is still drinking is trying to sell us something, trying to see if we can help them find a successful way to drink. The man I met that day was up to here with that. He did the same thing Bill did with Dr. Bob; Bill told Dr. Bob his story: "Every time I would take a drink, I would get drunk and I would mess up. I talked to a doctor in New York who told me I have a physical allergy to alcohol that produces a craving when I drink. That explains what was going on with me."

Dr. Bob probably thought, *The same thing has been going on with me.* Until then, Dr. Bob had thought of his drinking as a "sin." He was caught up in the old concepts of it.

The first thing you can do with your sponsoree is tell her your story. We make a mistake when we try to do something else. I did that at first, too. I once told a guy he needed to find God and take an inventory. He thought I was some kind of religious nut. Since I didn't begin by sharing my problem, I didn't allow him to see his problem.

Bill Wilson tells how he made the same mistake until he discovered that you first have to tell the person what it was like for you. If he asks *how* you did it, don't tell him at first. Don't get into that until he hears your story. You are putting yourself into the position to give evidence.

And Bill reminds us: you can't give away what you haven't got. There is no way you can witness—can give evidence—if you haven't had these experiences.

"The Doctor's Opinion" defines the problem; then "Bill's Story" shows somebody who had the problem and found the solution. This can give your sponsoree hope. In the next chapter, we will go into Step 2, which answers the question, "Where do you start?"

ASSIGNMENT FOR STEP 2

READING . . . FOR SPONSOREE

Ask the sponsoree to read Chapters 2, 3, and 4.

Have the sponsoree write a summary of no more that one page on each chapter.

DISCUSSION . . . FOR SPONSOR

Go over these chapters with your sponsoree. The sponsoree should be able to see and state that the "solution" is power, a Power greater than ourselves that can restore us to sanity.

Chapter 2, "There Is a Solution," describes the solution in detail. Chapter 3, "More about Alcoholism," discusses the insanity of the first drink. Chapter 4 is preparation for Step 3. Step 3 may be a problem; with the sponsoree's present understanding of God, it may seem an impossibility. So Chapter 4, "We Agnostics," introduces another way to look at a concept of God.

Give the sponsoree only a day or two on this assignment. It won't do him any good to sit for a month thinking he is powerless over alcohol and that his life is unmanageable! As the sponsor, your goal is to see whether the sponsoree believes in God; often you'll find the sponsoree is an agnostic.

Recognizing the Solution

My friend suggested what seemed to me a novel idea. He said,

"Why don't you choose your own conception of God?"

That statement hit me hard. It melted the icy intellectual mountain in whose shadow I had lived and shivered many years. I stood in the sunlight at last. *It was only a matter of being willing to believe in a Power greater than myself.*

—Bill W.,
Alcoholics Anonymous

STEP 2:
Came to believe that a Power greater than ourselves could restore us to sanity.

Nowhere in the Big Book does it tell how to work Steps 1 and 2. I hear people say they are working Steps 1 and 2. I don't think we really work Steps 1 and 2. (We work *on* Step 1 drinking in the bars!) In these Steps we are gathering information. Step 3 is the first Step we work.

Someone once asked Frank Buchman, the founder of the Oxford Groups, "Your program is a life-changing program: you surrender, you examine your sins, you confess and share, make restitution, and witness. Why would anyone undertake such a thing?" He answered in one word: "Calamity."

Steps 1 and 2 establish that calamity. The first two Steps are really preparation for the program. They are vital. They have to be done. As Bill Wilson found out, the program won't work without them.

All the first forty people got sober in the Oxford Groups. In the Oxford Groups, people focused on changing their lives, people from all walks of life who were dissatisfied with their lives or dissatisfied with their spiritual progress. (Interestingly, most were active members of churches.) They found that by using the Oxford Group principles they could make real changes in their lives.

When alcoholics started going to the Oxford Groups, the recovered alcoholics—Bill, Dr. Bob, and the rest of the first forty people—would go to their homes and spend a couple of hours talking with them and taking them through Step 1. They would tell their own stories and see whether the fellow realized he was powerless over alcohol. Then they would ask if they could come back in a few days. When they returned for the next visit, they wanted to be convinced that the prospect believed in God. They had to work the first two Steps with the person before taking him to an Oxford Group meeting.

So the third Step is really the first step in the program of recovery. In writing the Big Book, Bill Wilson realized it had to deliver the whole program. So he started with "The Doctor's Opinion" and the first four chapters to sell readers on "three pertinent ideas":

- that we were alcoholic and could not manage our own lives
- that probably no human power could have relieved our alcoholism
- that God could and would if He were sought

(Alcoholics Anonymous, p. 60)

These "three pertinent ideas" are essentially Steps 1 and 2. The first two Steps give us the information we need to make the decision to take Step 3: "Being convinced, *we were at Step Three,* which is that we decided to turn our will and our life over to God as we understood Him" (p. 60).

Three pertinent ideas:

- We were alcoholic and could not manage our own lives.

This is Step 1

- Probably no human power could have relieved our alcoholism.
- God could and would if He were sought.

This is Step 2

—Adapted from *Alcoholics Anonymous,* p. 60

You know, when we take Step 1, we are *already* powerless over alcohol: we have simply realized this truth. When we take Step 2 and come to believe that a Power greater than ourselves can restore us to sanity, there has *always been* this power, but we have just come to believe it, we have just become aware of the possibility. So those are the two realizations that help us take Step 3. Step 3 is the first Step in recovery.

And when we take Step 3 we make a decision—because a decision precedes all action. Steps 4, 5, 6, 7, 8, 9, and 10 are action Steps. All our improvement and progress come through the action Steps. We don't get improvement in our condition through Step 1: it's information. Step 2 is information. Step 3 is just a decision. But the Big Book promises results after Step 4, after Steps 5, 6, 7, 8, 9, and 10. The improvement comes about as we work the action Steps.

Remember: we don't actually work the first two Steps. We come to the conclusion that we are powerless. And through reading "The Doctor's Opinion" and "Bill's Story," we see why we are powerless. Through reading Chapters 2, 3, and 4, we become at least *willing* to believe that a Power greater than ourselves can restore us to sanity. So really instead of working Steps 1 and 2, we arrive at two conclusions. We don't have to *do* anything here. We were already powerless, and there always was a power, in spite of anything we might do. We just become aware of these truths. This puts us in the position to make a decision based on the information we have gathered, the awareness we have been given. These Steps are motivation for the decision in Step 3.

You couldn't start a person off at Step 3. He or she wouldn't realize the "calamity."

When your sponsoree understands from studying Chapter 2 that he or she is powerless, explain that the solution is *power*. Part of this power can be found in A.A. meetings, in listening to and talking with other alcoholics. This will give the sponsoree some hope. This will support him while he is working the program of action to bring about a spiritual experience.

A lot of therapeutic things will happen for the sponsoree just by being at the meetings. There is strength and power in the A.A. fellowship. I remember when I was first in the program. I would come home and my wife would ask me, "How was the meeting?" I'd say, "Fine." She'd say, "What did they do?" I'd say, "Nothing much. They drank a lot of coffee and smoked a lot of cigarettes. I can't wait to go back." (Today, with nonsmoking meetings, I'd have to say just, "They drank a lot of coffee—and some of *it* was decaf!")

There are two A.A.s: the fellowship that supports us and the program of action that changes us. One supports us; one changes us.

Support comes through the A.A. fellowship.

Change comes as a result of the A.A. program, that is, Steps 3 through 12.

In fact, some people don't even take the Steps; they just go to the meetings. That's *not* recovery, but it's true there's a lot of power in people being together. Dr. Jung told Rowland Hazard that people usually have their vital spiritual experience in conjunction with other people; this is one of the reasons churches are so successful.

And, you know, every time we introduce ourselves—"My name is Joe; I'm an alcoholic"—it's like taking the first Step all over again. And everybody says, "Hi, Joe!" Part of the power comes from the acceptance we have for each other. There is such a magical power there that a lot of people think it's recovery—it makes you feel that good—but it's support.

I sometimes hear people refer to A.A. as a "self-help group." I don't think A.A. is "self-help." After all, everybody there is "powerless." It's hard to think of it as a self-help group when everybody in the group is powerless! But it certainly is a *spiritual-help* group. There is something powerful about a group of people getting together for a common cause. I remember the meeting in the state hospital where I first said, "My name is Joe and I'm an alcoholic." Boy, that felt funny, but I felt better after I had said it. When I first started saying it, I didn't mean it. After a while, I did.

When your sponsoree comes to the conclusion that he is powerless, then he becomes ready to accept a Power greater than himself. If he is powerless, it will take a power beyond him to help. Part of that power is the fellowship.

BELIEVE • WILLINGNESS • INVESTIGATION

SIMPLE KIT
OF
SPIRITUAL
TOOLS

TWELVE STEPS

1 > 2 >> 3 > 4 >
5 > 6 > 7 > 8 >
9 > 10 > 11 > 12

Revolutionizes our whole
attitude toward life,
toward our fellows,
and toward God's Universe.

**Personality change sufficient
to recover from alcoholism**

OLD MEMBER

OLD MEMBER

Supports through EXPERIENCE

OLD MEMBER

NEW MEMBER

Supports through STRENGTH

OLD MEMBER

OLD MEMBER

Supports through HOPE

OLD MEMBER

OLD MEMBER

**Fellowship of those who suffer
the same problem**

He will know about the other power that is going to restore the person to sanity after working the Steps.

Your sponsoree will most likely not understand "sanity" the way we're using it. *Sanitas,* the Latin word *sanity* comes from, simply means wholeness. This is the sense in which Bill Wilson used it in writing the Steps and the Big Book.

Bill Wilson said many of us have good minds. We are able to see the truth about a lot of things in our lives. We wouldn't put our hands on a hot stove, for instance. But when it comes to alcohol, we're looking at an area of our lives where we're insane, where we can't see the truth about reality.

Your sponsoree may be thinking, *I'm productive, I have a good job, money in the bank, and some areas of my life that are under control.* He may be thinking he's not really crazy.

But you can point it out to him: when it comes specifically to alcohol, he *is* insane. If he doesn't see this truth, he is going to take a drink, which will set off craving in his body and obsessing in his mind, as he's learned in "The Doctor's Opinion." So your job is to help him see that in this one specific area, he is not whole; he is insane.

You can use the stories in Chapter 3, "More About Alcoholism." The stories of "the man of thirty," "Jim," and "Fred" all show the insanity just before drinking. The sponsoree might say, "I know I'm insane because when I drank, I did some crazy things." But that's not it either. When you drink and do crazy things, that behavior is caused by a drug called alcohol.

The insanity of alcoholism is the insanity that gets us just *before* we drink. It's a mental blind spot that makes us think that even though we have *always* drunk too much and got into all kinds of difficulties every time we have started drinking before, maybe this time we won't.

This is the *insanity of alcoholism*. We love the sensation; we think about the sense of ease and comfort we have felt before. We think a drink will make us feel so much better. We are so eager to see what it is going to do *for* us that we refuse to remember what it is inevitably going to do *to* us.

This is true of all kinds of drugs, all kinds of addictions. So this is the state of the mind we want to be delivered from.

We want the sponsoree to decide the Power referred to in Step 2 will do that. He doesn't even have to believe yet; he merely has to be willing to believe. This will bring it about. We should help him understand the difference between believing and knowing. Believing is the state of mind you have before you do something. Knowing is what you have after you do it—facts. We are asking the sponsoree only to be willing to believe that this power can restore him to sanity.

I remember the pain of putting my hand on the hot stove; I can't remember anything good that ever came of it.

Insanity is doing the same thing again and again—and expecting different results: if you keep on doing what you've been doing, you keep on getting burned.

So Step 2 deals with what the power is, what we want the power to do, and where the power comes from. The power comes from the fellowship and it comes from God. The power of God is a power we already have inside. When we work the Steps in the program of action, we will access that power. And that power will restore us to sanity. It's something we already have that needs to be discovered.

You may want to review Appendix II in the Big Book, page 569. Here we are told about a deep and effective spiritual experience that comes as the result of these Steps and that is sufficient to overcome the need to use alcohol or other mind-altering substances. There are two types: one we call a "spiritual experience," which is sudden; the other we call a "spiritual awakening." Bill's story includes his own dramatic spiritual experience. But experiences such as his *aren't* common.

The other type, which most of us have, is called a "spiritual awakening." The garden-variety spiritual awakening usually happens more gradually, maybe over a period of months. Often other people notice the change in our personality even before we ourselves are fully aware of it. But finally the person who follows this program realizes he has undergone a profound alteration of his reaction to life. Finally he is awake. And he is aware he didn't do this alone. At this point he has a concept of God. He identifies the power that altered him, that woke him up, as God. Up to this point he just had a willingness to believe; having worked the Steps, now he "knows."

I think it works kind of like shopping. We go to the store and there are so many choices available that we often choose a product because we remember someone told us it was good. Or maybe we recall a TV or magazine ad that we didn't realize we were even paying any attention to. We buy that product, and it works just fine. So the next time we don't wander all over the store; we walk right up and get the item that we know works. The suffering alcoholic is like that. Maybe he will be hurting enough and will believe us enough to try our simple program. If he does, he will soon *know* that it works.

The usual approach of most religions is to try to get people to accept a large, complex belief system. This program takes another approach. You can believe any way you want to believe as long as you are willing to believe. We do not attempt to prove God to people ahead of time. If you are willing to believe, and willing to follow this program, God will prove Himself to you. This is the approach laid out in Chapter 4, "We Agnostics." As Bill Wilson said, we have never seen it fail.

So the sponsoree starts out with his own conception. No matter how inadequate this conception of God is, it's where we all start from.

This is a basic principle, basic to learning anything: any time we try to learn something new, we have to start out with the concept that we have, and go from there. It's impossible to start anywhere else. I've had people tell me, "I don't believe in God." I say, "Well, that's where you have to begin."

We don't attempt to prove God to people. If you are willing to believe, and willing to follow this program, *God will prove Himself* to you.

Jesus told us to come to Him as a child. Most of us weren't allowed to start there even when we were children. We were expected to start at a "higher" level—wherever our parents were. They told us what we should believe about God.

I remember when I learned to drive a car. I had ridden with my father and I had watched him drive. I thought I could see what he was doing. I had a conception of what it was like to drive a car. So one day I got in the car with my conception, and I was surprised my conception was wrong. I hit the brake and it threw me up on the steering wheel; I turned the wheel too far to the right, and I had to bring it back too fast. My conception had been wrong. I made mistakes and corrected them, and I learned to drive. But first I had to be willing to try to drive even with my *inadequate concept* of what driving was going to be like.

I still have a different concept of driving than my wife. When we go places together, she wants me to drive using her conception of what driving is, especially her conception of navigating. She'll often say, "Why are you going this way? It's not the shortest way." I'll say, "Fewer lights." She has her way of going someplace; I have mine. Either one of us can get there.

But we have to start where we are. We have to start this journey—each of us—with our own conception of God, no matter how inadequate. We make mistakes and we learn from them.

Some of the most spiritual people I have met in this program are people who started off as agnostics. Many people who come to this program with a lot of beliefs have more closed minds and are not as willing to develop a knowledge of God through these actions. But, you know, their original belief system didn't keep them from being powerless over alcohol.

———

In Chapter 3, "More About Alcoholism," Bill Wilson relates the stories of "the man of thirty," "Jim," and "Fred." These are stories of people who, like ourselves, believed something that was untrue: that one day they would find a way to drink like other people. One exercise you should ask your sponsoree to do is to state what the character in each of these stories believed that was not true. Fred believed he could have a few highballs before dinner and no more; Jim believed he could drink safely if he mixed his liquor with a little milk. We have all been there! Your prospect has surely been there too and will recognize himself or herself in the stories.

In Step 1 we close the door 100 percent on this kind of thinking. We have exhausted all the possibilities of ever drinking sanely. When a person believes something that is not true, he will act on this delusion; and he will always, 100 percent of the time, run into the truth. A guy once told me, "Hell is the truth seen too late."

We are always powerless over alcohol. When we admit our powerlessness, we become available to the truth, and as Scripture teaches us, "The truth will make you free" (John 8:32). With this new freedom, we can turn the energies that we used for drinking to becoming sober, to recovering.

The human mind will rise to the challenge of finding a new way of life. Bill Wilson wrote, "As soon as a man can say that he does believe or is willing to believe, we emphatically assure him that he is on his way" (p. 47).

That's the taking-off point. Bill Wilson called Step 1 "the foundation"; he called Step 2 the "cornerstone" (p. 47). And he said that believing is the cornerstone of "the arch through which we passed to freedom" (p. 62).

Belief is the cornerstone, but we can't stop there. Next we have to make a decision and then take action. "We Agnostics" gives us a simple procedure. We become willing to believe; we decide to turn ourselves over to God; then we take certain actions. If we do this, we will know God. It never fails.

If the sponsoree has taken Step 1, he understands he has an allergy to alcohol, he understands that insanity is the state of the mind just before he takes the first drink. If you have guided him through Step 2, he will see the two sources of power that are the solution to his problem, and he should be willing to believe, to start with whatever concept of God he has. Then he is probably ready to make the decision to follow the procedures we will lay out for him.

There seems to be a momentum here, a dynamic, that once you get started with these, you will go on.

At this point all the sponsoree has to do is be willing to believe. She certainly doesn't have to define the power yet.

In the following Steps we are going to give her the procedures to follow.

ASSIGNMENT FOR STEP 3

READING . . . FOR SPONSOREE

Ask the sponsoree to read page 42 and the first half of page 43 in *Twelve Steps and Twelve Traditions*.

DISCUSSION . . . FOR SPONSOR

The sponsoree will need to understand the basic instincts of life.

When your sponsoree understands the problem, you can point out to him or her two choices: to go back to the problem, or to go to Step 2 to the Power.

If the sponsoree decides to go to Step 2, he or she is then ready to make the decision that is Step 3. This is often more effective when the sponsoree takes the Step with the sponsor, using the third-Step prayer found on page 63 of the Big Book.

Making an
Important Decision

There I humbly offered myself to God, as I then understood Him, to do with me as He would. I placed myself unreservedly under His care and direction. I admitted that of myself I was nothing; that without Him I was lost.

—Bill W.,
Alcoholics Anonymous

STEP 3:
Made a decision to turn our will and our lives over to the care of God *as we understood Him.*

To solve a problem, you have to ask three questions:

- What is the problem?
- What is the solution to the problem?
- What actions must I take to produce the solution?

The history of A.A. shows how we arrived at these things. In 1933 Bill got a clear statement of the problem from Dr. Silkworth at Towns Hospital. In 1934 Rowland Hazard brought back to Ebby Thatcher the solution to the problem as Dr. Carl Jung had described it to him. And Ebby told Bill about it at Bill's kitchen table in Brooklyn. The Oxford Groups showed them how to apply certain principles to bring about the solution.

When we use these three—the problem, the solution,

and the program of action—we solve the problem of alcoholism. Bill passed them on to Dr. Bob. And this is the message we pass on to others.

Step 3 says, "We made a decision to turn our will and our lives over to the care of God *as we understood Him.*" The term that the Oxford Groups used was *surrender.* Bill Wilson didn't think alcoholics would respond positively to that word. He was skilled in language and was always looking for a way to say things that wouldn't turn alcoholics off. He said the same thing, but the words are less pious, easier for alcoholics to respond to. Bill changed the words, but the idea, the concept, is the same. In Oxford Group literature, surrender was described as "the process by which we gave back to God that which he had so freely given us at our creation—will."

In the Big Book, we are asked, "Was it our self-esteem, our security, our ambitions, our personal relationships, or sex relations which had been interfered with?" (p. 65). These are the basic instincts of life. These are the things that make up what we call "self."

In *Twelve Steps and Twelve Traditions,*[2] Bill Wilson expands on the idea of the "basic instincts of life" that he had first introduced in the Big Book:

> Creation gave us instincts for a purpose. Without them we would not be complete human beings. If men and women didn't exert themselves to be secure in their persons, made no effort to harvest food or construct

---

[2]The "Twelve and Twelve" isn't about sponsorship; it isn't really about how to work the Steps. The "Twelve and Twelve" is not meant to substitute for the Big Book in telling us how to take the Steps, but it expands our understanding of them and shows us how Bill was thinking as the length of his sobriety increased.

Since Bill lived in New York City and was familiar with the theater and with stage plays, he uses the metaphor of an actor trying to run the whole show to describe self-will in the Big Book (see pages 60–61). He expands on it in the *Twelve Steps and Twelve Traditions.*

shelter, there would be no survival. If they didn't reproduce, the earth wouldn't be populated. If there were no
social instincts, if men cared nothing for the society of
one another, there would be no society.

Our basic, God-given instincts motivate us to function
and often dominate us. They make us do everything, both
good and bad. As Bill Wilson explained,

> . . . these desires—for the sex relation, for material
> and emotional security, and for companionship—are
> perfectly necessary and right, and surely God-given.
> Yet these instincts, so necessary for our existence,
> often far exceed their proper functions. Powerfully,
> blindly, many times subtly, they drive us, dominate
> us, and insist upon ruling our lives. Our desires for sex,
> for material and emotional security, and for an impor-
> tant place in society often tyrannize us. When thus out
> of joint, man's natural desires cause him great trouble.
> Practically all the trouble there is.

All our troubles come from these basic human instincts.
All human troubles come from these basic desires out of
control. Bill goes on to say that nobody has ever been able
to be perfect in their relationship with them:

> No human being, however good, is exempt from
> these troubles. Nearly every serious emotional prob-
> lem can be seen as a case of misdirected instincts.
> When that happens, our great natural assets, the
> instincts, have turned into physical and mental liabil-
> ities. (*Twelve Steps and Twelve Traditions,* p. 42)

Step 4 is our vigorous and painstaking effort to discover
what these liabilities in each of us have been, and are. We
want to find exactly how, when, and where our natural
desires have warped us. We wish to look squarely at the
unhappiness this has caused others and ourselves. By
discovering what our emotional deformities are, we can

move toward their correction. Without a willing and persistent effort to do this, there can be little sobriety or contentment for us. Without a searching and fearless moral inventory, most of us have found that the faith that really works in daily living is still out of reach. (pp. 42–43)

OUR BASIC INSTINCTS

If men and women didn't exert themselves to be secure in their persons, made no effort to harvest food or construct shelter, there would be no survival . . .

These are our security instincts.

If they didn't reproduce, the earth wouldn't be populated . . .

These are our sex instincts.

If there were no social instincts, if men cared nothing for the society of one another, there would be no society . . .

These are our social instincts.

These desires, for the sex relation, for material and emotional security, and for companionship, are perfectly necessary and right, and surely God-given . . .

We are supposed to have them.

Yet these instincts, so necessary for our existence, often far exceed their proper functions . . . They drive us, dominate us, and insist upon ruling our lives . . .

All the troubles we have come from our basic instincts out of control.

—Adapted from *Twelve Steps and Twelve Traditions*, pp. 42–43

We need to understand that God placed all these motivations in us—for companionship, self-esteem, sex, and so on. These things make up self-will. When you fulfill one of these basic instincts, there is an automatic reward—pleasure. But the pleasure is so good that we often overdo it. It's the overdoing that makes what we call "defects of character." We become dishonest, selfish, self-seeking, frightened, and inconsiderate. So our character defects are nothing but a misuse of one of these necessary basic instincts.

The purpose of Steps 4, 5, 6, 7, 8, and 9 is to enable us to discover and get rid of these deformities. To get there, we must make the decision of Step 3.

The Big Book notes that "any life run on self-will can hardly be a success" (p. 60). Your sponsoree needs to gain an understanding of what "self-will" is.

Self-will has to be a strong drive—because life is based on it. God made this powerful force. And the same force that makes it possible for us to succeed as individuals and as societies also is the reason, when it is defective, that people are in prisons.

We are not going to get rid of self-will. Only God's will can overcome it. We will turn it over to God and He will, through these Steps, remove the things that block us. If we do this, we are going to be relatively happy. At least we are not going to drink alcohol—because that is "self-will run riot" (p. 62). The whole program—not just Step 3—is a process of correcting the will. Step 3 is the *decision* to work Steps 4, 5, 6, 7, 8, 9, 10, 11, and 12.

When you work this Step with a new person, you should sit down with her and explain to her what she is being asked to turn over:

- "our wills," which are thought processes, and
- "our lives," which are actions.

Our actions are the results of our thought processes. God not only gave us will, He also gave us the intelligence to carry out the actions that are required by our will. Will and intelligence are the things that set us apart from other creatures.

If you look out your window, you will see two types of things: natural things, which are the result of God's will, and human things, which are the result of human will. Only these two forces—God and human beings—have will.

When you have a product that won't work right, the best place to take it to get it fixed is back to the people who made it in the first place. When we have a problem with human will, we can only take it back to the Creator who created it in the first place. So Step 3 is a very simple concept. We surrender and say, "I can't fix it; I'm powerless," and we take our will back to its Maker and say, "I've decided to let you fix it." That's letting go. But the decision is going to have to initiate some action on our part to do what we have to do to bring our sobriety about.

In helping another person to take Step 3, you should go over the first two Steps, and make sure he or she sees the alternatives. We can't follow two different sets of directions. If we want God's will, we have to give up our own will.

In the early days of our program, when it was still dominated by the nonalcoholic people in the Oxford Groups, Steps 1 and 2 were qualifying steps. Recovering alcoholics would first come to the candidate's house and see if he was convinced he was powerless over alcohol. If they were satisfied he was, they'd say, "Can we come back and see you in a couple of days?" When they came back the second time, they'd see whether he believed in God. If he qualified on both counts, they would invite him to a meeting of the

Basic Instincts of Life That Create Self

SOCIAL INSTINCT	SECURITY INSTINCT	SEX INSTINCT
COMPANIONSHIP: Wanting to belong or to be accepted.	MATERIAL: Wanting money, buildings, property, clothing, etc. in order to be secure in the future.	NATURAL: In accordance with human nature; normal.
PRESTIGE: The power to command admiration, coveted status.	EMOTIONAL: Based upon our needs for another person or persons. Some tend to dominate; some are overly dependent on others.	DESIRE: To long for; to wish for; to ask for.
SELF-ESTEEM: What we think of ourselves, high or low.		REPRODUCTION: Act of reproducing. Giving rise to offspring.
PRIDE: An unjustified opinion of oneself, either positive (self-love) or negative (self-hate).	AMBITIONS: Our plans to gain material wealth, or to dominate, or to depend upon others.	AMBITIONS: Our plans to gain material wealth, or to dominate, or to depend upon others.
PERSONAL RELATIONSHIPS: Our relations with other human beings and the world around us.		
AMBITIONS: Our plans to gain acceptance, power, recognition, prestige, etc.		

Oxford Groups where they would start him off on their first step, which became our Step 3. He would make his decision, and they would pray with him.

Carl Jung told Rowland Hazard that the spiritual experience usually occurs when people are working together. God most often works this change through other people. So they thought it was effective to take Step 3 with another person. (See page 63.) If you are sponsoring someone, and you take Step 3 with him, you will at least know that he has taken it.

Sometimes you'll hear someone in the program say, "Well, I took Step 3 and turned my life and will over to God, but I'm still having a lot of problems in my life. I can't figure out what is wrong." The key here is to understand that you don't turn your life over to the care of God in Step 3, you just make the decision to do it. The decision requires further action.

My wife and I went to the race track one day; I spotted a horse on the program named Summertime. I told Loubelle, "I'm going to bet on that horse." But I went to the window and placed two dollars here and two dollars there until I had spent about $20. She said, "Aren't you going to bet on that horse?"

I said, "Nah, I'm through. I'm not going to spend another penny."

He came in and paid $140! I could have gone down to the window and said, "Look Mister, I didn't bet on the horse, but I made a decision to." He'd have said, "We don't pay on decisions; we pay on what you put up."

It's the same thing here: we make a decision to turn our will and our lives over to God, but the Big Book says there are certain things that are blocking us from God and that we have to go to work immediately to remove these things. These things are resentments, fears, and our guilt and remorse about the past—our "defects of character."

Our basic instincts have made us dishonest. We do something dishonest; then we fear that somebody is going to find out. This fear dominates our lives and blocks us off from God. So since we want God to direct our lives, we have to get the fear out of our minds.

When our basic instincts are out of control, the least little thing that somebody says or does hurts us. Then we have a resentment. This resentment blocks us from God. So we can see how these things emanate from our defects of character—from the inside out.

All human problems come from our trying to satisfy one of the desires that make up our basic instincts. We have to learn not only to get rid of these kinds of reactions and responses to our basic needs, but also how to keep them from coming back.

We have a process that works to minimize them on a daily basis. This is why the Steps work. As Bill Wilson observed, our problems are with life: "Liquor was but a symptom of our problems" (p. 64). Our problem is we don't know how to live.

As you work with sponsorees, remember that Step 3 is the very first Step in the recovery process. Step 1 gives us information; Step 2 gives us information. Even Step 3 doesn't have any permanent effect if we don't follow it immediately with action. The program is going to pay off based on the action we put into it.

The first real therapeutic progress comes after Step 4. Then each of the following action steps brings more relief. Most alcoholics are not satisfied with their actions. They have tried making pledges to do better; they have tried everything they can think of because they don't like their lives. But changing our lives is not a matter of thinking only. It is a matter of taking action.

Most alcoholics don't like their lives.

Changing our lives is not a matter of thinking only.

It is a matter of taking action.

The Big Book says that Step 3 is just a decision and has no permanent effect unless followed by "vigorous action" to remove the things that are blocking us (p. 63). The following Steps—4 through 10—are where we actually put the money on the race.

In recent years, treatment centers have had a lot of influence on the program. Some treatment centers have clients do Steps 1 through 4 and then release them and tell them to go home and find a sponsor. But if you do only these Steps, you have only done one action Step.

The Steps are a process that relies on sequence and momentum. In the early days of A.A. they did the Steps quickly. When I was new in the program, we were given six weeks to work the Steps. And we were given assignments to work every day. Everybody was required to do them. Nowadays we have people who don't do it this way. We have people who have the required "desire to stop drinking," but they haven't worked the Steps. They can be a part of the fellowship, but they aren't really a part of *recovery* until they work the Steps.

Remember that all the people in our fellowship groups are not really alcoholics. (Bill Wilson discusses three types of drinkers in Chapter 2; see pages 20–21.) I think we have some people in the fellowship who are "hard drinkers." They don't need to have a spiritual experience brought about by working these Steps; they can just quit drinking. They aren't really alcoholic—because an alcoholic can't do that. They don't usually stay; they just come in and out of our fellowship. But they don't have a message to share. Sometimes we have a nice response to working Step 3, but we haven't started to recover yet. Bill Wilson writes that as soon as we take Step 3, we should take Step 4 "at once":

> Though our decision was a vital and crucial step, it could have little permanent effect unless at once followed by a strenuous effort to face, and to be rid of, the things in ourselves which had been blocking us. Our liquor was but a symptom. (p. 64)

That makes good sense. You need to move your sponsoree along pretty fast, because she's in pain. The rhythm and momentum are very important. If she sits around and stares after she has taken Step 1, she will only get more confused and more worried. Of course, as I've said, you have to work with each person on an individual basis, but you need to keep the sponsoree busy and keep her moving. If your sponsoree seems capable of moving a little faster, let her go on and make progress.

The first two Steps are really preparation. Steps 3 through 12 are the program of action: the way we find the power. When your sponsoree gets ready to start applying the actions, you should just move him right on through them—bam, bam, bam, bam. Keep the momentum. Let it happen.

I've heard people say they are taking one Step a month. And I have heard people who have been going to meetings a year ask when they should start taking the Steps. They are just prolonging their suffering! What's the use of sitting around for a long time brooding over the fact that you are powerless over alcohol? They are sitting around A.A. meetings, getting miserable, but now they can't even have the relief they used to get from drinking! They are *really* miserable.

But if you get through Step 1 and admit you are power-less, and then through Step 2 and believe that a Power greater than yourself can restore you to sanity, you are going to *want* some momentum. Most people are going to want to get going and get some sanity, some power.

Rowland Hazard took Ebby Thatcher to his house for two weeks to work the Steps. When he felt Ebby had moved far enough along, he took him to Sam Shoemaker's Calvary Mission to work with other alcoholics. Bill worked the Steps at Towns Hospital in 1934. Read pages 12 and 13 of the Big Book to see the momentum with which Bill worked the Steps.

The Big Book suggests that if we are comfortable doing so, we get down on our knees with the person and read the Step 3 prayer with him:

> God, I offer myself to Thee—to build with me and do with me as Thou wilt. Relieve me of the bondage of self, that I may better do Thy will. Take away my dif-ficulties, that victory over them may bear witness to those I would help of Thy power, Thy love, and Thy way of life. May I do Thy will always!
>
> (*Alcoholics Anonymous,*
> p. 60)

It is important for your sponsoree to understand that he hasn't really turned his life over to God at this Step; he has merely made the decision to do so. The actual turning over comes about with the action Steps that follow. The decision has to be followed by action!

Self-Will

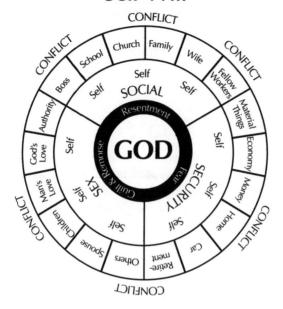

God's Will

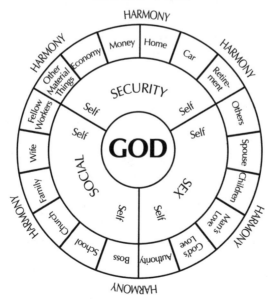

ASSIGNMENT FOR STEP 4

READING . . . FOR SPONSOREE

Ask the sponsoree to read pages 63–71 in the Big Book and pages 42–43 in *Twelve Steps and Twelve Traditions.*

DISCUSSION . . . FOR SPONSOR

When you are satisfied that your sponsoree has taken Step 3, you give the next assignment: Step 4. Step 4 is gathering and putting together the information for doing Steps 5 through 9. And you can't really work a good Step 10 if you haven't done a solid Step 4.

When you guide your sponsoree through Step 4, use the rhythm illustrated in the Big Book. That is, let him or her just do the inventory of "resentments," and complete that, and go over it with you. (First, explain to your sponsoree what a resentment is. As a sponsor, you will need to understand resentment, and fear, and guilt and remorse well enough to help your sponsoree get to the truth underlying these things.) Then have your sponsoree do the inventory of "fears" and go over that together. Then do the "sex conduct" inventory with him or her the same way, thoroughly and honestly. And finally, have him or her do the inventory of "other harms."

If you have been working with a person for a week or ten days, set aside about a week to do this Step. You can't just say to the sponsoree, "Go start on your inventory," because it might take him a month—maybe two months. Create a schedule by saying something like, "We are going to work on 'resentments' for two days." Then do the other inventories similarly, with a schedule for each one that doesn't allow the sponsoree to skimp, but that moves him or her along at a good pace.

Taking Inventory

I ruthlessly faced my sins . . .

—Bill W.,
Alcoholics Anonymous

STEP 4:
Made a searching and fearless moral
inventory of ourselves.

It seems to me there's been a lot of confusion about how to do an inventory.

Some people say to write out your life story. That's not what the Big Book says. You don't get any additional information by writing out your life story[3]—because you already know it or you couldn't write it. What you need to do is find, and face, the facts of your life.

Step 4 is extremely important because it is the Step where the person gathers the information used to work the rest of the program:

- What wrongs have you done to others? You find this in Step 4.
- What defects of character do you have? You find this in Step 4.
- What shortcomings? Step 4.
- What problems with other people are you going to rectify in Steps 8 and 9? Look at your Step 4.

---

[3]The Big Book does say we tell someone all our life story, but that's in Step 5.

For the rest of the process, through the Steps that follow, it all goes back to Step 4.

Bill Wilson dramatizes the inventory process by comparing it to a business. He reminds us a business that doesn't take an inventory will go broke. He explains what a business inventory is and says that we are to take a similar inventory of our lives.

He's teaching us something by showing us how it is like something we already know; he's drawing an analogy between a business and a life. Jesus did this. When Jesus talked to shepherds, he told stories about sheep herding; when he talked to farmers, his stories were about things familiar to farmers.

As Bill Wilson put it, just as a business will go broke if it doesn't take a good inventory, if we don't take a thorough and honest personal inventory, we will go broke too. For alcoholics, this means getting drunk!

A business inventory is	A personal inventory is
fact-finding	searching
fact-facing	fearless
truthful	moral

He explains that a business inventory is "fact-finding and fact-facing," an effort to "disclose damaged or unsalable goods" (p. 64). In Step 4, your sponsoree's task is to do the same—discover "damaged and unsalable goods"—in his or her character, in his or her life. The Step reads "searching and fearless . . . ," and this is fact-finding and fact-facing; "moral" is truthful. Our "stock in trade" is, of course, ourselves. What damaged goods are on the shelf today, right now? If the sponsoree does his inventory this way, he will learn the truth about himself. He'll learn what things are blocking him from God, what things are making him drunk.

I like to say, "We are not what we *think* we are, but what we think, we *are.*" Everyone—not just alcoholics—can suffer from distorted thinking. This is important because our lives each day are based on our thoughts each day. That's our stock-in-trade.

"As a man thinketh, so is he."

—Proverbs 23:7

In fact, we're not talking about alcohol anymore. Alcohol has nothing to do with it anymore. We are talking about how we live our lives. That's why more than two hundred groups helping people with many kinds of problems can use this program. I've seen people in other programs who use these Steps more effectively to bring about the changes in their lives than do many A.A.s. I know many of them who have beautiful spiritual lives. In Al-Anon, Step 1 is the admission of being powerless over "people, places, and things." That's pretty all-inclusive. That's a pretty big Step. It surely requires you to live on a spiritual plane.

There is no mention of alcohol in Step 4. In fact, there is no further mention of alcohol after Step 1. In A.A. and in all the Twelve-Step programs, we are trying to find a *new way of life.*

So Step 4 is looking at our "business." The sponsoree is going to list his or her defects of character and analyze them. In many discussion meetings, I've heard people say, "Don't analyze, utilize." But we're told to analyze in the Big Book: " We have listed and *analyzed* our resentments . . ." (p. 70; italics added).

We analyze to get to the truth, the "exact nature" of our problem. When a detective comes to a crime scene, he analyzes the evidence to get to the truth. When we have a resentment, it is because we do not see all the truth. If we could see the truth of a situation, we wouldn't have a resentment.

The inventory is a beautiful and efficient process of finding the truth. We're not looking for good or bad. We're looking for truth. A sponsor can be very helpful in a person's getting to the truth—because the sponsor has been through this process herself.

The inventory is not a life story; your sponsoree doesn't have to put down the year he graduated from high school or anything like that. On page 65 in the Big Book is a plain and precise inventory. Your sponsoree will do inventory forms based on this example.

There's one problem, though: the example Bill Wilson gives us there is already filled out, so the sponsoree may ask, "What procedure did he use to complete it?" The instructions are in the Big Book, but they are extremely brief: "In dealing with resentments, we set them on paper. We listed people, institutions, or principles with whom we were angry" (p. 64).

It's hard for a sick mind to analyze a sick mind. And you can't analyze in your head. You have to write it down.

The Big Book shows the example of an inventory of resentments. You'll show your sponsoree how to inventory her resentments. Then she'll do the same for fears. And the same for sex conduct and for other harms done to others.

You will need to explain what resentments are, and perhaps what fears are. As the inventory form will show, we can't have a fear unless one of our basic instincts has been threatened. When we have fear, "self" is endangered or threatened.

Manifestations of Self

SOCIAL INSTINCT

COMPANIONSHIP: Wanting to belong or to be accepted.

PRESTIGE: Wanting to be recognized or to be accepted as a leader.

SELF-ESTEEM: What we think of ourselves, high or low.

PRIDE: An excessive and unjustified opinion of oneself, either positive (self-love) or negative (self-hate).

PERSONAL RELATIONSHIPS: Our relations with other human beings and with the world around us.

AMBITIONS: Our plans to gain acceptance, power, recognition, prestige, etc.

SECURITY INSTINCT

MATERIAL: Wanting money, buildings, property, clothing, etc., in order to be secure.

EMOTIONAL: Based upon our needs for another person or persons. Some tend to dominate; some are overly dependent on others.

AMBITIONS: Our plans to gain material wealth, or to dominate, or to depend on others.

SEXUAL INSTINCT

ACCEPTABLE: Our sex lives as accepted by either society's, God's, or by our own principles.

HIDDEN: Elements of our sex lives that are contrary to either society's, God's, or our own principles.

AMBITION: Our plans regarding our sex lives, either acceptable or hidden.

SELF

WRONGS

RESENTMENTS

Feelings of bitter hurt or indignation that come from having rightly or wrongly held feelings of being injured or offended.

FEARS

Feelings of anxiety, agitation, uneasiness, apprehension, etc.

HARMS OR HURTS

Wrong acts that result in pain, hurt feelings, worry, financial loss, etc., for others and also for self.

The reason we inventory our sex conduct is this: our sex conduct is one of the deepest ways we hurt one another. The sex instinct is one of our strongest basic instincts. It has to be to make us reproduce and "take dominion" over the earth, as Scripture says. Sex is satisfying, so satisfying and pleasurable that people overdo it and are often dishonest about what they have done. This frequently puts us in conflict with others.

Once the sponsoree takes inventory of harms done through sex conduct, he will add to the list the names of people he's harmed in any other way. These will be people toward whom, when he thinks of them, he feels guilt and remorse. Guilt and remorse block us from God just like resentments and fears. When we feel guilt and remorse, our minds are being directed by the persons we have harmed.

(Also see pages 64 and 76 in the Big Book in regard to Step 8—because the work done here is groundwork for Step 8.)

INSTRUCTIONS FOR USING THE INVENTORY FORMS . . .

Included in this chapter are four forms for inventories of resentments, fears, sex conduct, and other harms done to others, all drawn from the example on page 65.

We do a column at a time: top to bottom completely. I've found it's essential that the person do the first column first, top to bottom, for instance, listing resentments. Then the second column: "We asked ourselves *why* we were angry" (p. 64). In this column, the person tells why he was or is angry, top to bottom, at each of these persons, institutions, or principles. Then we go back to the top, to the third column. In this column, the person will note which of the instincts was threatened by the event in the second column. The Big Book says about this column: "In most cases, it was found that our *self-esteem, our pocket books, our ambitions, our personal relationships (including sex) were hurt or threatened"* (pp. 64–65; italics added).

Guide your sponsoree to do each column from top to bottom, completing the first column, then the second, and so on. Emphasize that it's not effective to fill out the inventory moving across horizontally on each line.

It's almost automatic for a person to want to work across—since we read and write from left to right—but you can show your sponsoree how to fill out these columns vertically from top to bottom, completing each column before going on to the next one.

One of the secrets of this kind of inventory is that you don't have to analyze the information yourself: you put the information in vertical columns, and the inventory will "analyze" it.

You can encourage your sponsoree by telling him or her,

Exhaust your mind of all the resentments you have by asking,

"Who or what am I resentful toward?"

Then in the second column,

"What did they do that made me resentful?"

Then in the third column,

"Which of my natural, God-given instincts was threatened?"

Finally in the fourth column,

"What is the exact nature of my wrongs?"

Review of Resentments

COLUMN 1	COLUMN 2	COLUMN 3	COLUMN 4
I Am Resentful At: I list people, institutions or principles with whom I am angry.	**The Cause:** I ask myself why I am angry, what did they do to me to cause the anger?	**Affects My:** On my grudge list I set opposite each name my injuries. Was it my self-esteem, my security, my ambitions, my personal, or sex relations that had been interfered with?	**Where Had I Been:** • "Selfish" • "Dishonest" • "Self-Seeking and Frightened" • "Inconsiderate"? Which of the above character defects caused me to do what I did, or caused me to want to hold on to the old resentment, even though I may have done nothing to cause it?

Your sponsoree will look at one thing at a time, recording what he sees while his mind is on that one topic.

When we make out the first column, we are usually surprised at how many resentments we have. When we are just thinking about them, we are only able to see one resentment at a time; but when we list them this way, we will be able to see them all at once for the first time.

Then the sponsoree will do the second column. He will start to realize, "It's not really those people in the first column who made me mad; it's what they did."

Now we come to the third column. We know from reading the Big Book and *Twelve Steps and Twelve Traditions* that these are the basic, natural instincts of life. And we know they are God-given and there is nothing intrinsically wrong with them. Social instincts, security instincts, and sex instincts—everybody has them. They're the characteristics that make us human. These desires are very important to us. You cannot have a resentment unless one of these basic instincts has been affected. If we have a resentment, one of these basic instincts has been threatened, endangered, or negatively affected in some way.

So in the third column the sponsoree looks to see which of the basic instincts was affected by the person in Column 1 and the event in Column 2. Column 3 records this. Once the sponsoree gets to this column, he doesn't really have to look back at the name in the first column anymore. He is now interested in what part of himself was threatened.

Here we come to realize the importance of a sincere and complete Step 3. The ability to work this part of the program of recovery depends on the person's having a strong commitment to the Step 3 decision. This is why it's important for the sponsoree to understand the basic instincts before taking Step 3. Often the sponsoree will see that more than one basic instinct was threatened by each act or event.

Now we can see why we were angry. Many people—

most people, in fact—have a problem with anger. But, you know, you have to understand the problem before you can do anything to solve it. Sometimes we may say, "I'm going to quit being angry." We usually can't just do that—because anger is a natural response to one of our basic instincts being threatened. Your response to it is based on your spiritual fitness. When I am spiritually fit, you can do just about anything you want to threaten one of my basic instincts and it won't bother me.

Bill Wilson says, "If we were to live, we had to be free of anger" (p. 66). Often when we're angry, we're angry about something that's not true. If you get to the truth of the situation, the truth will set you free. There is no way to know the truth about something and still be angry. So the truth is what we are searching for. The truth can be an elusive thing though.

We are searching for the truth—because the degree of truth in our lives determines the quality of our lives. When we are living a life based on self-will, we have to spend all our time protecting our basic instincts. This is where the anger, which is a lie, the fear, which is a lie, and all our behaviors that hurt other people come from—from our trying to protect ourselves in response to these basic survival instincts. In the "Twelve and Twelve," Bill Wilson calls this the root of all human problems: "These basic instincts which are God-given and necessary finally far exceed their proper function" (*Twelve Steps and Twelve Traditions,* p. 42). We are looking at the damage of the past, the damage of living our lives based on self-will.

On the bottom of page 64 in the Big Book, Bill explains "spiritual malady." When a person is spiritually ill, God can't work in that person's life. That person has effectively blocked himself or herself from God. Many people say, "God is blocked out." But I think of it as God's being blocked in—because I believe God is *in* every man, woman, and child.

When our basic instincts are deformed, when we are trying to live a life run on self-will, over a period of time we develop in our minds certain thoughts and responses that block God in. Human beings work from the inside out: from spirit and mind to our actions. When we have taken our mind and our actions and lived a life with "self" at the center, we have blocked God in. A person who is spiritually sick has blocked God in. We made the decision in Step 3 to place God in the center of our lives, but we can't use Him until we get rid of the things in our minds and our actions and relationships with other people that block us from God. Steps 4 through 9 serve to remove them, to remove the wreckage of the past.

Living to satisfy your basic instincts produces resentments. Your material and emotional security always feel threatened, and you always feel afraid. And if you are living with these fears, you are going to hurt a lot of people and have a lot of guilt and remorse. So obviously if you are living a life based on your basic instincts only, you are always going to be in conflict with God, with yourself, and with other people. So the purpose of Step 4 is to list these deformities of the basic instincts so you can look at them and analyze them.

We can be ill physically, mentally, and spiritually. The Big Book says that if we can get well spiritually, we will recover physically and mentally also. So we are going to get well from the inside out.

In Step 3, the sponsoree made a decision that God—not the basic instincts—direct his or her life. In Steps 4, 5, 6, and 7, your sponsoree will look at thought processes. In Step 4, he will put them on paper. This is a beautiful step to take. For the first time, the person can actually look at his thinking—get a picture of it. He has been going through so many problems in his life—he's been driven so hard by his instincts for economic security and social needs that he has been living in reaction to this person and that person. He's driven by self-will, yet he doesn't really have an identity. He's pretty confused at this point. After he finishes Step 4, he might not have the identity he would like, but he will have a starting point. He will begin to know himself.

So, once the sponsoree has listed the threatened basic instincts, he will have three columns. Now these are the only three columns illustrated in the Big Book. For some reason, the things we are really looking for are not shown in the illustration. (Maybe the page wasn't wide enough!) But we are given the instructions for finding them on page 67: "Referring to our list again. Putting out of our minds the wrongs others had done, we resolutely looked for our own mistakes. Where had we been *selfish, dishonest, self-seeking, and frightened?*"

Now the sponsoree can forget about the name of the person, institution, or principle, forget about the cause, even forget about the basic instinct. Now she will ask what *she* did wrong. In all these resentments, your sponsoree will have been wrong in some way. But she may not even know it because her culpability has been covered in her perception by her focus on what *someone else* did.

It takes some reflection. In most cases, the sponsoree will find that he did something based on self-will, something responding to a threat to his basic instincts, and the other person did something in retaliation. But he won't see this until he gets the fourth column written down and looks at it.

There is great freedom in doing this. Because once we see and can own what we did, we may realize that the other people might not even have done what they did if we hadn't done what we did.

Once we see the truth of these situations, it will often be impossible to resent the other person. In many cases, we will owe this person an amend.

A resentment is a way we can transfer the blame to someone else. And that protects our self-esteem. But once we
see our fault in a situation, we don't have to hold that
person "hostage" anymore—or let the person "live rent-
free in our head" anymore, as Al-Anons say.

Most people think that the inventory is going to help
them analyze things. And they want to analyze as they go
along, as they write things down. I want to stress again the
importance of doing each column vertically. The process
itself will provide the analysis if you separate these ideas
into columns and do the columns one at a time. The sponsoree enters the items from top to bottom, one column at
a time. Then, when he reads the inventory form across for
the first time, he sees the truth.

Sometimes I've told people who seemed to be having a
hard time with their inventory, "I want you to make a list
of everybody and everything you resent. That's all I want
you to do." I don't even let them do the second column until
they have completed that first column. Then I show them
how the rest of it works.

When they have completed all the columns, I say, "Now
we're going to read it across, and you will see a complete
picture." Now, for the first time, he or she can see why the
person listed under "resentments" in the first column did
what he did—often because of something that appears in
the fourth column.

So when the sponsoree starts an inventory, say the
"resentments" inventory, he puts all the names down first in
column 1. Then he lists the causes in column 2. In the next
column, column 3, he lists the basic instincts that were
threatened. Then we get down to what we are looking for:
which character defect did *he or she* have? This is column 4.

In column 4, we get to the "inside" and find out—were we

dishonest?
selfish?
self-seeking?
frightened?
inconsiderate?

We are working from the outside in, but the resentment started from the inside out. It was a character defect of our own that hurt the other person.

We have many different types of character defects. The ones I've mentioned above are like the basic colors. You know, you can take the basic colors, red, blue, and yellow, and make an almost infinite number of shades by combining them in different ways. In the same way we "mix" our character defects. Greed, for example, is a mixture of basic defects—as are jealousy, envy, and others.

Everyone has character defects. Why? Because everyone has the basic instincts. They will always be there because they're part of our human make-up. They are natural and God-given.

We can look at our social instincts, for instance—our desire to be accepted by other people, our desire to be respected, and maybe our desire to lead. These desires can make us selfish; they can make us dishonest; they can make us self-seeking, fearful, and inconsiderate.

We all have the basic desire for material and emotional security. Everybody has trouble with these instincts, too. These instincts can make us selfish, dishonest, self-seeking, fearful, and inconsiderate. The same is true with our sexual instincts.

We know of only one person who was ever born on this

earth who was perfect, and even He battled with them. Jesus came to the world to show us how we should live. Once, near the time of His death, just before He was about to be executed, He had a bout with resentment. He said of His sleeping disciples that they couldn't even watch with Him for one hour while He prayed. He suffered with fear and asked God if there was some way the bitter cup could be taken from Him. Here we see how very strong these instincts are. But He overcame them. How did He do it? He prayed, "Not my will but thine be done." He surrendered. He gave up self. Later He asked that all the people who had let Him down, and even the people who tortured and killed Him, be forgiven. In responding in this way, He demonstrated to us how we should behave toward the basic instincts of life. He took them on, lived with them, and overcame them.

The Big Book is based on these principles. All of us have the same basic desires. We don't see or can't admit being wrong; it's easier to resent the other person for what we perceive as his wrongs toward us. We keep on resenting him until, after a period of time, we have managed to transfer all the blame to him. We have to cover up what we've done—to protect our self-esteem. Resentment is a defense mechanism, you know, and we may go for a long time retrying a case in our mind, convincing ourselves that the other person was wrong because we think that this will make *us* right.

So when we look at the inventory form all the way across, and we see what we have done, it doesn't take away what the other person did. But we don't have any *power* over what the other person did—we do have power over what we did or what we do in the future.

Regardless of whether we were right or wrong, we've still turned our life over to that person. When you hold a resentment against someone, you give your power to that person. You let her affect the way you feel. If you sincerely look for your part, for your fault, at the very least your character defect will be that you were "inconsiderate." ("Inconsiderate" is always an out!) The other person may be a sick person, and you were not considerate enough of this. You didn't allow him to be spiritually sick. If you can see that you were at least inconsiderate, it will free you.

We'll say more about this when we get to Step 10, but we have to have consistent ground rules. This is one: no matter what happens, I'm going to find where it is my "fault." In some situations we have to look hard for it, but "inconsiderate" can be our last resort. It will be there to free you.

It doesn't matter what the other person did or how sick the other person may be, because you can't do anything about that. But if you can find which one of your character defects kicked in, you can work on it. That's why you want it to always be your "fault."

The reason I want it always to be my fault is because I have some tools now to do something about me. If it remains the other person's fault, I am trapped again. I can do nothing about the other person. I am in a losing situation. But if it is my fault, I have a way of working out of it.

We might have done nothing more than be inconsiderate. Even if the other person is more wrong than we are, that's not our business. But being inconsiderate is our business, and we can take care of that.

———

What about those who have wronged us? The Big Book offers this guidance:

> We turned back to the list for it held the key to the future. We were prepared to look at it from an entirely different angle. We began to see that the world and its people really dominated us. In that state, the wrong-doing of others, fancied or real, had the power to actually kill. How could we escape? We saw that these resentments must be mastered, but how? We could not

wish them away any more than alcohol. This was our course: We realized that the people who wronged us were perhaps spiritually sick. Though we did not like their symptoms and the way these disturbed us, they, like ourselves, were sick too. We asked God to show them the same tolerance, pity, and patience that we would cheerfully grant a sick friend. When a person offended we said to ourselves, "This is a sick man. How can I be helpful to him? God save me from being angry. Thy will be done" (pp. 66–67).

Lots of times a person who hurts us is in a stressful situation that we don't know about. They strike at us out of that bad place. Or we may have done something to threaten that person, and we don't realize it. Sometimes even things we mean in a positive way will threaten somebody. You can get another degree, or you can step up in your job. You improve yourself, and that's part of your life. Some people may be threatened by that. This is the way human nature is. We are learning the truth about how human nature works as we work this Step.

ACTING AND REACTING . . .

We live in a world of conflict. We perceive it as coming from other people, but much of our conflict originates in our own minds. It may seem that others are against us, but it's usually coming from within ourselves.

We have already determined that our thoughts come first and then our actions follow, but if we can get a pattern of actions going, they can sometimes influence our thoughts.

One of the very first things Al-Anon teaches is not to *react* to everything. That's about choosing not to be threatened.

You don't have to react to everything that comes your way and looks like it might be a threat. Al-Anons learn to practice this way of acting—especially important for people living with somebody who is still drinking or using drugs.

If you practice not reacting, your life becomes more orderly. You don't even have to understand it at first. You just have to practice. This works with raising children; it works with the people you work with. You know, everything that gets to be a big deal gets that way because somebody involved *overreacts*. Lots of times, people want you to jump in emotionally and get embroiled with them.

We are often fearful in a situation that if we don't do something to "fix it" right now, it won't be fixed. But sometimes *nothing* is the best thing that we can do. Sometimes we need to do something *right now;* sometimes we need to think it over.

We are looking for a balance, and it will come from practice using these tools. Once we start getting well, the Promises tell us that "we will intuitively know how to handle situations that used to baffle us" (p. 84).

When I have a resentment, it is an indicator for me that I am trying to cover something up about myself. I look at the fourth column of the inventory and see what I'm trying to cover up, and I can see it right away. It takes developing skills over a period of time, and practicing in Step 10, but Step 4 is where we learn the basics of it.

Step 4 is the kindergarten of the rest of the Steps. You want your sponsoree to work this Step carefully and thoroughly because it's going to provide what he needs to work the rest of the Steps. In the Big Book, Bill Wilson lists the *people:* Mr. Brown, Mrs. Jones, my employer, my wife; then he lists the *causes:* his attention to my wife, etc.; then which of the basic instincts of life was *affected:* self-esteem, security, etc. But remember Bill didn't have the fourth column. The defects in the fourth column come directly from the basic instincts.

You know, our defects affect other people and they retaliate. If we can get rid of our defects of character—dishonesty, selfishness, self-seeking, fear, lack of consideration—the basic instincts will be healthy. If our basic instincts are healthy, and anybody does strike us, it won't hurt. Chances are, if our basic instincts are healthy, people are not going to attack us—because we are not going to do so many things that would provoke them.

Resentment is an inside job.

Happiness is an inside job, too.

The new person who is taking Step 4 doesn't realize all this yet. But he doesn't have to understand. Maybe he won't understand it until he has worked all his Steps. Maybe not until he starts sponsoring somebody else. All he needs to do now is understand the process of doing the inventory and be willing to do it thoroughly and honestly.

Resentment is not unnatural. It serves a purpose or God wouldn't have given it to us. Fear is not unnatural. Without it we wouldn't be able to live very long because we would be heedless of real, life-threatening dangers. Guilt and remorse are also useful. Without them, we would have even less consideration for others; we would run over people. But we have to use these things properly, and we never become perfect at it. Alcoholics have all these things out of order. They are going around and around in a big circle. What we are trying to do here—we're not trying to become perfect—what we are trying to do is to round up these character defects, and get them in some semblance of order so we can have a measure of contentment and happiness. So that at least we will not have to drink alcohol.

Resentments are constructive at least to the extent that they make us active and competitive. Sometimes when a person does something and gets "ahead" of us, it strikes one of our basic instincts. It can make us want to achieve something ourselves, to do something constructive. That's probably why God gave it to us. The key is that, instead of letting the resentment fester, you can use the same energy to accomplish something healthy. Otherwise, if you sit with it bottled up inside you, it becomes destructive.

Even if something is not our fault—and sometimes it's *not;* someone may have done something unprovoked—we still have a way of dealing with it. Even when we can't find where we were really at fault, we can find where our reaction was at fault. Perhaps our sense of self was offended in some way; this may have caused us to feel fearful. But in this program we have tapped a power that enables us *not* to have to react in a fearful way to every negative action directed toward us.

As we are able to turn our basic instincts over to God, they become less and less powerful in our lives. When God is directing your life, you don't need to be protecting yourself all the time. Your fear will go away.

One of the great advantages we have in life is that as we learn what makes *us* tick, we also learn what makes others tick, what makes them act and react as they do. They are humans, too! We have to let people be people, and not be threatened by everything they do. We must be just as free as we can be. We are looking for freedom: freedom from character defects, personal freedom. When we find it, we don't have to go around being threatened. We just put things in perspective and go on down the road.

Step 4 is the foundation for the rest of the action Steps. If the inventories are done well, the following Steps will just fall into place.

In Step 5, we learn even more about what makes us tick, and as a result, we learn more about what makes others tick!

Review of Resentments

COLUMN 1	COLUMN 2	COLUMN 3	COLUMN 4
I Am Resentful At:	**The Cause:**	**Affects My:**	**Where Had I Been:**
I list people, institutions or principles with whom I am angry.	I ask myself why I am angry, what did they do to me to cause the anger?	On my grudge list I set opposite each name my injuries. Was it my self-esteem, my security, my ambitions, my personal, or sex relations that had been interfered with?	• "Selfish" • "Dishonest" • "Self-Seeking and Frightened: • "Inconsiderate"? Which of the above character defects caused me to do what I did, or caused me to want to hold on to the old resentment, even though I may have done nothing to cause it?

Review of Fears

COLUMN 1	COLUMN 2	COLUMN 3	COLUMN 4
Who Or What Do I Fear: I list people, institutions, or principles that I fear.	**The Cause:** What are they going to do to me? Am I perhaps going to jail? Am I going to lose something with material value? Will it result in divorce? Will it destroy a personal relationship? Might I lose my job, etc.?	**Affects My:** On my fears list I set opposite each name the part of self that is affected. Is it my self-esteem, my security, my ambitions, my personal, or sex relations that have been threatened?	**Where Had I Been:** • "Selfish" • "Dishonest" • "Self-Seeking and Frightened" • "Inconsiderate"? Which of the above character defects caused me to do what I did, or cause me to want to hold on to the old fear, even though I may have done nothing to cause it?

Review of My Own Sex Conduct

COLUMN 1	COLUMN 2	COLUMN 3	COLUMN 4
Who Did I Hurt:	What Did I Do?	Affects My:	Where Had I Been:
		Which part of self caused me to do what I did? Was it caused by the social instinct, the security instinct, or the sex instinct?	• "Selfish" • "Dishonest" • "Self-Seeking and Frightened" • "Inconsiderate"? Which of the above character defects caused me to do what I do to harm another?

ASSIGNMENT FOR STEP 5

READING . . . FOR SPONSOREE

Ask the sponsoree to read chapter 6, "Into Action" (pp. 72–75), and to review the first five Steps (p. 59).

DISCUSSION . . . FOR SPONSOR

In Step 4, your sponsoree undertook the inventory to try to find out important things about himself. Now he has to "admit to God . . . and another human being the exact nature" of what he has found. The sponsor is often that other human being.

Your job is to improve the sponsoree's understanding of what he has found. Chances are that in doing the inventory, the sponsoree will see a lot of things about himself he has never seen before. And he undoubtedly will miss some important and useful insights because he is emotionally involved with the information.

As the sponsoree begins Step 5, you will want to make sure he or she understands the basic instincts: that they are part of human life, part of our basic make-up, and that they are God-given and therefore good. Our plan is not designed to get rid of them, but rather to adjust them, to use them as they were meant to be used.

Learning What Makes Us Tick

My schoolmate visited me, and I fully acquainted
him with my problems and deficiencies.
—Bill Wilson,
Alcoholics Anonymous

STEP 5:
Admitted to God, to ourselves, and to
another human being the exact nature
of our wrongs.

Step 5 is simple. The sponsor's job in Step 5 is to "improve
on" the information the sponsoree has found in Step 4.

Even though the columns in the inventory were written
down one at a time from top to bottom, as a sponsor you will
study the completed inventories, reading every line across.
(It's helpful if the sponsor has taken this kind of inventory
as part of his or her own recovery—but not absolutely necessary.) You will go to the first column of the "resentments"
inventory and read the name—though this is no longer
important. Then you read what the person did and trace this
across to the third column, where the sponsoree has indi-
cated which of the basic instincts was threatened.

"If you would lift me, you must be on higher ground."
—Emerson

You won't make any changes in the sponsoree's information in the first two columns. You can't really improve on these. These two columns show what the sponsoree remembers about what happened—how he saw it. But there will be some things in the third column he will have overlooked or imperfectly understood: perhaps some basic instincts were affected that he didn't recognize. You should point these out to him.

The major changes will be in the most important column—column 4. This is where the information we've been looking for will appear, so we want this to be correct. There will probably be a good many changes and additions in this column. As you talk to him about these changes, you should make sure that the sponsoree agrees with your evaluation. And that he accepts the new results.

The Step 5 process is not a confession. Instead, it's an attempt to find the "exact nature" of the wrong, that is, the origin of the wrong, the characteristics of the wrong. Remember that all our problems come from character defects developed as a result of our basic instincts responding to what we perceive as threats.

Not only are we helping the person see the "exact nature" of his wrongs, but we're also beginning to teach her a process she should use daily for the rest of her life: Step 10. She will need to do this every day to analyze problems that arise, but, of course, she won't be able to come to you every time. So you're not only trying to help her get rid of the old things that are blocking her from God and from sanity but also teaching her how to maintain her new way of life using Step 10.

You know, there are many things about which it's hard for us to see the truth because of our defenses, because we are quick to rationalize. So it's easier for another person to see the truth clearly.

I've often had people come to me with situations where the truth was obvious to me because I was not directly involved. A few years ago, a woman who had been in the program for quite a while came to me with a situation. She had a resentment. She said she had done something trying to help someone at her church who had a drinking problem. Some of the people at her church—the minister and some of the leaders—were offended. They had criticized her, and she was really hurt by it. She said they had done it for no reason whatsoever. She believed that she had done nothing that deserved their censure. But to me, an outsider in the situation, her offense against them was obvious. She had done something: she had threatened them when she helped the alcoholic. Her pastor had surely felt that as the leader of the church, he was the one who was supposed to help the man. Remember that Jesus was a threat to the hierarchy of the church because of the good things he did! They were so offended that they went to the Romans and had him done in.

Human nature being what it is, we're often going to threaten people. Even our constructive living is going to threaten them. It will hurt their egos and their self-esteem sometimes. So people may retaliate against us for doing right. It's human nature.

A recovering alcoholic getting sober in his or her circle of friends is often a threat to them. It's impossible to live on the face of the earth without coming into conflict with other people. That's why we describe our character defects as normal things out of whack. The basic instincts of life—the desire for companionship, to have self-esteem and the esteem of others, the desire for material security—these desires are so strong they can make us dissatisfied and selfish. Every human being is sometimes dishonest. The desire for material and emotional security will sometimes make you dishonest, selfish, self-seeking, frightened, and inconsiderate. No human being in the world can live without the basic instincts that drive us. The fulfillment of these needs is what motivates us in our lives.

How does our program suggest we respond to people when we realize that we have hurt them even though we're doing the right thing? It's easy. We can always classify this kind of situation as our having been "inconsiderate."

Remember the woman whose minister was angry at her? The woman simply wasn't going to choose not to help the alcoholic who asked her for help, but when the church people responded by being angry at her, she had to let them be as they were. She had to understand them because she understands the basic instincts of life and so she doesn't feel resentful toward them. She understands what's going on with them. She can't do anything about how they respond. That's the price she has to pay for helping someone.

We just go on and do the next right thing; we don't respond to the predictable criticism—not even with resentment. Because we know something about human nature.

If she reacts to them, then they react again, and a fight goes on. But we don't have to respond this way because after we have done our fourth column, examined the exact nature of our wrongs, we will know what makes people tick. We have seen what we are like, and we know that every human being is pretty much just like we are. Since we know this, we can get along better with people; we can even allow them to be wrong. When we inventory an unacceptable situation and can't find any other of our character defects to bring it back to us so we can take some action, "inconsiderate" may be the defect we're looking for. It's simple: we can always be more understanding, more considerate.

And the point of doing this, even when we haven't been dishonest, selfish, self-seeking, or fearful, is so we can take responsibility for the situation. We want to do that. We don't want the blame for the situation to be on the other person. We can't have the blame on the other person. We want it to be on us. Always before this we have been trying to place the blame on another person or on a situation, but now we want it to be "my fault." Because once we can see that we were inconsiderate or at fault in some way—even a small way—we can do something about it. But we can't do anything about changing someone else. We have the tools now to work on ourselves. We are free.

> To be free from a problem, I have to own it. If I have an emotional problem, it comes from some kind of misdirected instinct.

Sometimes the other person is just flat out wrong. Bill Wilson explains this very well in the Big Book:

> We realized that the people who wronged us were perhaps spiritually sick. Though we did not like their symptoms and the way these disturbed us, they, like ourselves, were sick too. (pp. 66–67)

I can just tell myself, "That is a sick person." It's like a card game: I'd rather play with my cards. It's disarming. Remember: a person who has to pass the blame is usually a very frightened person.

That's part of the process of getting rid of resentments. As your sponsoree puts these resentments down on paper in Step 4, as he analyzes them in Step 5, he begins to get to the truth.

You know, when we see the truth of what we have been doing, we often feel ridiculous. We don't like to think of ourselves as being that dumb. Because even though a resentment sounds pretty good rattling around in our head, once we put it on paper, it looks double dumb. And most of these resentments will be gone just by writing them down and looking at the truth of them.

Sometimes there are some deep-seated resentments that we aren't able to just analyze and leave behind. For these we use prayer. Most people you sponsor will have at least one of these: a deep-seated thing that's hard to get over.

When you're working with someone who is having trouble with a deep-seated resentment, you may want to refer to pages 551–552 in the Big Book. The passage begins, "I've had many spiritual experiences since I've been in the program, many that I didn't recognize right away, for I'm slow to learn and they take many guises." The speaker goes on to describe a tough resentment she had against her mother. She tells about finding a magazine article in which a clergyman made this suggestion: "If you have a resentment you want to be free of, if you will pray for the person or the thing that you resent, you will be free. If you will ask in prayer for everything you want for yourself to be given to them, you will be free. Ask for their health, their prosperity, their happiness, and you will be free . . . Do it every day for two weeks." I use this in all the groups I do on resentment.

We sometimes think that if we stay angry with someone, he will eventually come around to seeing how wrong he was. But this is silly; he isn't going to. You can't hold a thought and make another person change.

In Steps 4 and 5, we are seeking the truth about a situation. If you have a resentment, it is a lie. But the truth will set you free. A resentment is usually a way of trying to transfer the blame to somebody else. Until we write an inventory, we see it as a "one-two-three" problem; but after our inventory, we can see that it is really a "four-one-two-three" problem. What's in column 4 was the first element in the problem.

It's hard to look at column 4 because that's us. If we can put the blame back on the person listed in column 1, it can be someone else's fault. Our natural instincts tell us not to look at what's in column 4 because we have to protect ourselves.

> Walt Kelly, in his Pogo comic strip, said it well: "We have seen the enemy, and he is us."

Here's the Step 5 process, the process of working with a sponsoree on the inventories done in Step 4:

- Make an appointment with the sponsoree to go over the inventories of "resentments," "fears," "sex conduct," and "harms done to others."
- Read the inventories before the meeting, and think about the questions you have. (With some experience, you'll be able to see things pretty quickly and won't need to go over them much ahead of time.)
- Concentrate on the fourth column of the inventories; you're primarily trying to help the sponsoree with the fourth column because Step 5 asks us about the "exact nature" of our wrongs.
- What's important are the character defects: dishonesty, selfishness, self-seeking, fear, and lack of consideration of others (see page 69 of the Big Book). Your job is to help the sponsoree "improve on" her moral inventory.
- Remember that the purpose of the inventory and analysis is to bring the sponsoree to what she will work on in Steps 6, 7, 8, 9, and 10.

When we do Step 5, we are not much interested in columns 1 and 2 anymore; column 3 is interesting to us because God created the basic instincts and gave them to us for our survival. But recall that in Step 3 we made the decision to turn these things over to God—because "self" cannot cure "self."

So the work of the fifth Step is in column 4. The other columns are now simply by-products of the inventory process.

Now here's a reward: once the sponsoree understands column 4—in what ways he's been selfish, self-seeking, dishonest, fearful, and inconsiderate—he'll be able to get along with people better because he'll know where they're coming from most of the time. He won't be able to be too judgmental though—because he discovered this by looking at himself, at *his own* shortcomings.

We don't go around analyzing people, but we know what makes people tick. We've had to learn a lot about it to start getting sober!

Anger and resentment are things that all people have to express some way. I've heard people say, when they realized how much trouble these reactions were causing them, "I'm just going to *stop* being angry and resentful." I don't think that's possible. We're not going to be able to stop feeling these things until we get to the root causes of them. Anger and resentment are caused by one of our basic instincts having been threatened and we are, as the Big Book says, "burned up" (p. 65).

But we will come to see how we are allowing others to control us through our own reactions. They are controlling our minds, what we are thinking, and therefore our actions. We are trying to take charge of our lives.

> If we want to take charge of our lives, we have to conquer self—from the inside, not the outside. If we can conquer ourselves, we will have conquered the whole world.

If we continue to work on developing these tools we've been given, we will be able to live almost resentment-free. We are bound to have a relapse every once in a while, but compared to the way we used to let other people's actions control us, we will be able to live free. Through the application of Steps 4 through 9, we who were emotional cripples, we who let everyone else run our lives, come out of this program with a superior way of living.

Some days when I am feeling spiritually fit, I notice people who don't even drink and am amazed by how sick they seem to be. They get upset over the least little thing that happens in traffic, in the grocery store, anywhere. Since they don't drink, I wonder how they are ever going to get well. They don't even know they are sick. We can be thankful we don't have to live that way anymore.

> Selfish means "I want this for me even though it may keep you from having it." Selfish is the opposite of generous. Self-seeking is trying to put yourself up front, in the limelight.

The key to Step 5 is to remember that it's not a confession; it doesn't matter whether the sponsoree has stolen something—or even if he has stolen something twenty times. What we are trying to get to are the character defects in Column 4. The key to gaining relief here is whether these character defects, when we become able to name them, are *objectionable* to us. If they are not objectionable, we will not be willing to give them up as we must do in Step 6. As sponsors, we can help the sponsoree come to recognize how stupid, how small, how objectionable these things are.

I've seen some Step 5s that took six or seven hours, that were a hundred pages long. I remember my own inventory: for every resentment I had, I found I had done something based on what my basic instincts told me was a threat to one of my needs. And someone had retaliated and hurt me. Never had anyone just come up to me unprovoked and done something that caused me to have a resentment.

We can get rid of all the resentments and fears we've had all these years that have caused us to drink and mess up our lives. But what's most important is getting rid of the character defects that brought them about in the first place. Because if we don't get rid of these character defects, the resentments or fears will all come back again.

So as your sponsoree goes through her inventories of resentments, fears, and harms done to others, looks at the ones she thinks are stupid and objectionable, and prays about the rest of them, she finds a process to get rid of them. But what about the future? If she doesn't get rid of the underlying character defects, she's going to have a bunch more resentments or fears or guilt and remorse next week, next month, next year.

The purpose of the process is to help the sponsoree get rid of character defects so she can live free of resentments, fears, and guilt and remorse. She probably won't get one hundred percent free immediately, but she will make progress. At least it won't be necessary for her to drink. But the sponsoree doesn't—and we don't—have to stop there. We can use this program to go to any level of progress we choose.

Through Step 5 we find the "exact nature of our wrongs." The exact nature, the inherent nature, of our wrongs is always going to be a character defect. And they're "wrong" because they effectively block us from God. When the blocks are removed, we begin an exciting journey of growth and change.

ASSIGNMENT FOR STEPS 6 AND 7

READING . . . FOR SPONSOREE

Ask your sponsoree to read Chapter 6, page 76, and to review his or her inventories, with special emphasis on the fourth column.

DISCUSSION . . . FOR SPONSOR

As a sponsor, you can go over the specific details in Steps 4 and 5. You can share your understanding of the exact nature of the wrongs; you can ask your sponsoree to commit to begin immediately to work Steps 6 and 7. This means if she wants these things removed, she has to do certain things. These are *action* Steps.

You can encourage your sponsoree by speaking to her about some of the changes you've made in your own life, how you made them, what those changes have meant to you. This will encourage the person to make the necessary changes. But after you have got the person through 3, 4, and 5, the work is pretty much up to the sponsoree.

Some people make improvements more quickly than others, but by this time you should be able to see changes in the person you're sponsoring. This depends a lot on how much time you're spending with the person, but if you're working with her as you should be, you should be able to see some changes—often before she sees them herself. If you're not seeing some results, you should talk with her to see if you can find out what she's not doing.

You're aware of the sponsoree's shortcomings because you've gone over Step 5 with her. You've seen in black and white what your sponsoree needs to be doing. So you can monitor her progress, see the subtle changes that maybe the sponsoree can't see. And you should let her know she is making progress. If she is not making progress, you should share this with her too.

Growing and Changing

I . . . became willing to have my new-found Friend take [my defects] away, root and branch. I have not had a drink since.

—Bill W.,
Alcoholics Anonymous

STEP 6:
Were entirely ready to have God remove all these defects of character.

STEP 7:
Humbly asked Him to remove our shortcomings.

When Bill Wilson wrote the Steps, he began, as we've said, with the tenets, or steps, of the Oxford Groups:

- Surrender (our Step 3)
- Examine your sins (our Step 4)
- Share and confess your sins (our Step 5)
- Make restitution (our Steps 8 and 9)
- Ask for God's guidance (our Step 11)

He had added "admit you're licked," which became Step 1. But he had begun to think the Oxford Group steps needed to be expanded for alcoholics. He felt that although the tenets of the Oxford Group had been successful bringing about change in many people's lives, alcoholics needed to change more.

Bill is thought to have said the Oxford Group's tenets had "loopholes that alcoholics were jumping through." He had that on his mind. But when he began, he probably had no idea what he was going to add or take away.

So he sat in bed that night in Brooklyn and wrote "How It Works," Chapter 5 in the Big Book. He had been trying for weeks to get started.

He believed the first four chapters of the Big Book were preparation, that it was now time to get down to telling the new alcoholic how to go about recovery. But he felt inadequate. So, he said, he prayed for guidance, and he picked up his pad and pencil. In thirty minutes he had written the Steps and the rest of "How it Works." When he went back and numbered them, he discovered there were twelve.

Bill Wilson had seen that the Oxford Group tenets had to be expanded to accommodate the special needs of alcoholics. He believed—he knew—that alcoholics need more *power* and more *strength.* And these are in the changing Steps: 6, 7, and 10.

Steps 4 and 5 have put your sponsoree in a position to start some work. Through them, as the Big Book says, " . . . we have put our finger on the weak items in our personal inventory" (p. 72). When he has worked Steps 4 and 5, your sponsoree can see and understand something that is real, and he can make some changes—perhaps for the very first time. You know, every alcoholic I've ever met has tried to make changes. He has tried to control his drinking, but that didn't work. He has tried to quit drinking; that didn't work either. Then in A.A. he finds out his problem is not drinking; his problem is living. He learns he has resentments, fears, and guilt and remorse. He accepts that. In A.A., he learns that having those feelings isn't the "exact nature" of the problem. He has to go deeper. Finally, when he works Steps 4 and 5, he puts his finger on the things he has been looking for all his life.

His "character defects" should become *objectionable* to him. With the insights from the process of Steps 4 and 5, he comes to see "the exact nature" of his wrongs. For change to come about, these things have to become objectionable. Bill wrote, "Are we now ready to let God remove from us all the things which we have admitted are objectionable?" (p. 76)

You know, human beings usually resist change. We won't make changes unless we understand that the change is vitally necessary. We can get used to using what we have no matter how inadequate.

So in Step 6, we see these things—our character defects—as objectionable, and we become willing to let go of them. We're ready for Step 7. These two Steps are not like Steps 1 through 5, one after another: I think of them as side by side. When something becomes objectionable, we can replace it with something else.

SELF-WILL	GOD'S WILL
Driven by our basic instincts (security, social, and sexual instincts), we become	With our new way of life, we become
. . . dishonest	. . . honest
. . . selfish	. . . unselfish, generous
. . . self-seeking	. . . humble
. . . frightened	. . . courageous
. . . inconsiderate	. . . considerate, kind

We use prayer to bring this change about:

My Creator, I am now willing that you should have all of me, good and bad. I pray you now remove from me every single defect of character that stands in the way of my usefulness to you and my fellows. Grant me strength, as I go out from here, to do your bidding. Amen. (p. 76)

We have to realize that the character defects in our lives have usually come from long practice. After you have practiced a behavior for ninety days, you own it. Your sponsoree —like everyone else—has just gone along, not evaluating what he has picked up, listening to other people, taking shortcuts.

We don't think anything about habits as we acquire them. But once we own them, we practice them in our lives. Your sponsoree will get his life back by practicing new habits and new ways of thinking he gets from working this program. He hadn't done an inventory of himself before; he didn't know his "stock-in-trade." Now, having done an inventory, he has some authentic information. He can change his stock-in-trade! This is the thrilling part of the program. Now he has the tools to do something about it.

He says about one of his character defects, "This is objectionable, so I'm not going to practice it anymore." But if he's not going to practice it anymore, he's going to have to practice something in its place. The thing he's going to practice in its place is usually its opposite. This is very difficult, but we know it can be done: we have seen others do it.

Change is not just getting rid of something. Change is replacing the things we want to get rid of. We know nature abhors a vacuum. We know the principle that if something is removed, something else takes its place. We can't remove a character defect unless we replace it with something we are short of. We know that if we practice dishonesty, we are going to have low self-esteem. We know the only way to get over dishonesty is to practice honesty. The only thing that can replace dishonesty is honesty.

As you practice honesty over a period of time and get

fewer resentments, less anger, less fear, less guilt and remorse, and your life gets better, you get along better with people. Your self-esteem goes up, and you find the rewards for honesty far exceed the results you were getting from dishonesty. You cannot know this until you have practiced it. We have to be willing to give up the old to gain the new. Until we give up the old, we can't know the value of the new. Change means taking a chance.

Once your sponsoree starts practicing her new habits, she will realize how much better things are than they were when she was practicing her old habits. But she can't know this until she practices the new ways.

Steps 6 and 7 are the changing tools. I think the greatest obstacle is the fear of change. Everybody wants something new, but most people don't want to give up what's old. And they want to make sure they are right. But when we start something new, we don't know what lies ahead. We don't know whether we are going to be successful.

The key to success with Step 1 was willingness; the key to Step 6 is also willingness, and the key to Step 8 is going to be willingness. Willingness is a state of mind that allows us to believe (Step 2), allows us to decide (Step 3), and allows us to act (Steps 4 through 10). We have to *believe* we are going to change, we have to *decide* to change, and we have to *act* to change. This is what we have to do. Nobody can do it for us, and our willingness is the key.

How do we become willing? Step 4 gives us vital information that will motivate us to want to change. Although we have always resisted change, now we see the possibility of being successful. Once we enter into the change, it becomes an exciting thing. When a new alcoholic starts working this program and starts to see what his or her new tools are making possible, it is always exciting.

Most people do not know we continue on this path of growth for our whole lives. It is not just about initial sobriety and overcoming the glaring and damaging things in our lives. We make the initial changes and our lives become wonderful. But there will be things we have continued to hold onto that are going to become objectionable to us. We keep going to another level. It's like a hot-air balloon: the more ballast we are willing to throw out of the basket, the higher we can go. These principles are about so much more than just not drinking. They can continue all our lives to increase the quality of our lives. We can live better than most people ever dream possible.

Bill Wilson says that Steps 6 and 7 separate the "men from the boys" because in them we come face to face with ourselves. It is always simple: What do we want to gain? What are we willing to give up?

At Step 1, there is enormous relief, and we get it again at Step 6—if we are willing to do the challenging things that are required.

Both are based on willingness. Step 1 makes us willing to go through with the following Steps, and Step 6 gives us the willingness to go through Steps 7 through 10. If we're willing to try it, we'll get the results. It's like putting up money on a winning horse at the track. The guy who puts up $100 gets more back than the guy who was only willing to put up $2.

Steps 6, 7, and 10 are simple tools like picks and shovels. With a pick and a shovel, you don't need the complex instructions you do for more complicated kinds of tools. The person working these Steps just has to come face to face with himself. His progress is based on what he does. There are not a lot of instructions.

God respects our free will. We can do what we want to do. If we insist on it, He will let us use our free will until it kills us. If we have the will to give it up, we can get something better.

Self-will is dishonest, self-seeking, and resentful. God's

will is honest, giving, and forgiving. And it is already within us. We have these good qualities within us, but we have practiced and used the bad ones. When we begin to use the good qualities, we begin to feel better and we use the bad qualities less and less. After a while they will almost disappear. This is the choice that our quality of life is based on.

This change won't come about overnight. It takes years of prayer and practice. Some people think they will just turn everything over to God, God will zap them, and all at once they will have a great change. But it doesn't work that way for us. We have to work at it. How did we get sick? We worked at it. We become what we practice. How do we get well? We work at it. We become what we practice.

Where you start is not where you finish—so start somewhere.

With these two principles in Steps 6 and 7, our potential for growth is unlimited. But we tend to become complacent and waste some of this potential. I see it as a waste of this program that many people come in, gain some semblance of recovery, and just stay there; they don't try to grow any more. They use the program to keep from drinking, instead of for *living*. The principles in this program enable us to go to any level we want to. They enable us to live better than most people. Sobriety is just the beginning!

From a sponsor's viewpoint, there's not a lot of help you can give the sponsoree at this point. But having gone through the inventory process with the sponsoree, you know a lot about the person. The person also knows you and has confidence in you. You can start growing together.

Remember: these two steps are tools like a pick and shovel, you just show the sponsoree where the handle is. He's got to use it.

ASSIGNMENT FOR STEPS 8 AND 9

READING . . . FOR SPONSOREE

Ask your sponsoree to read chapter 6, and to study pages 76–84. Study the names of people, institutions, and principles listed in Step 4 with which he or she has had conflict. Ask your sponsoree to add names as needed.

DISCUSSION . . . FOR SPONSOR

The goal of sponsorship is to guide a person through the Steps to recovery. The best material we have for this is the Big Book; we should use it throughout sponsorship. It is one of the sources of our authority.

You'll notice that the Big Book devotes more space to Steps 8 and 9 than to any of the other Steps. You need to help your sponsoree with more direction and more detail at these Steps. Making amends can't be rushed into without thoughtful preparation and guidance.

I believe the key for successful sponsorship here is a thorough knowledge and understanding of pages 76 –84. You should read this passage carefully before working with your sponsoree.

The Big Book outlines the process clearly; you will be able to help the sponsoree by following the Big Book.

The Big Book notes that the sponsoree should have done a great deal of the work for Step 8 already: " . . . We have been thorough about personal inventory . . . We have listed and analyzed our resentments . . . We have listed the people we have hurt by our conduct, and are willing to straighten out the past . . ." (p. 70). And, it continues, "We have a list of all the persons we have hurt. We made it when we took inventory" (p. 76).

In other words, if your sponsoree has followed the instructions, when he or she gets to Step 8, half of it will be done already. When your sponsoree begins Steps 8 and 9, the list that he or she needs will have been completed in Step 4. That's the way the Big Book says to do it.

Straightening Out the Past

[My friend Ebby and I] made a list of people I had hurt or toward whom I felt resentment. I expressed my entire willingness to approach these individuals, admitting my wrong. Never was I to be critical of them. I was to right all such matters to the utmost of my ability.

—Bill W.,
Alcoholics Anonymous

STEP 8:
Made a list of all the people we had harmed, and became willing to make amends to them all.

STEP 9:
Made direct amends to such people wherever possible, except when to do so would injure them or others.

Making amends is a process:

- we make a list of people we have harmed,
- we become willing to make amends to them, and
- we make direct amends wherever possible, except when to do so would injure them or others.

Your sponsoree goes back to Column 1 on the "resentments" list from Step 4 to begin.

When he did Step 5, he found the exact nature of his wrongs. He learned that the origins of his difficulties—the exact nature of his wrongs—appeared in column 4 of the inventory form. He learned that in many instances it all began with his actions. He learned his character defects grew out of his basic instincts. He saw that he had done something based on his instincts—column 3. He had reacted to something, and the person retaliated—column 2.

This being so, instead of resenting the person in column 1 of the "resentments" list, he probably owes this person an amend. So he puts most of these people on his amends list. He will also have people from his "fears" list, people he is afraid of facing. Usually having done something based on one of his natural instincts (and his character defects) has placed him in a position of experiencing fear. The only way to get over the fear is to face the person and set that wrong right.

The sponsoree also goes over the first column of his sex-conduct inventory, and his inventory of other harms done to others. He puts the names of people he has harmed on his new amends list.

The sponsoree will get some names off the first column of each of the four inventories. All of these go on the amends list, even though he may not yet see how he's going to make the amends.

When the sponsoree has finished this list made up from the Step 4 inventories, you should sit down with him and ask him, "Are there other people you have harmed?" He should analyze this, too. If other people occur to the sponsoree, he should not put down just the name alone, but follow through all four columns with them, too, so he can see his involvement and what he did. Then he will own that amend. The names are not enough information; he shouldn't take a shortcut.

Your sponsoree won't have to make amends to all the people on his list. Remember the woman whose minister and others were disturbed because she had helped the alcoholic? She doesn't owe them an amend. Your sponsoree only adds to the list people whom he has harmed.

You can see that Steps 8 and 9 have potential pitfalls: the sponsoree might make amends to the wrong person, or make amends that he doesn't need to make. Here a sponsor can be very helpful; as a sponsor, you can help your sponsoree determine what he needs to do.

Step 8 is simple:

half of it is already done in Step 4,

and the key to it is willingness.

There are two basic things to do in Step 8:

- make the list, which is essentially already done, and
- become willing to make amends.

Willingness is the key. In *Twelve Steps and Twelve Traditions*, Bill Wilson wrote that freedom may come more from the willingness than from the actual doing of it:

> . . . if a willing start is made, then the advantages of doing this will so quickly reveal themselves that the pain will be lessened as one obstacle after another melts away. (pp. 77–78)

Once we are genuinely willing to make the amends, we can be free whether we have actually made them or not. Willingness is the key.

Remember this is not a "self-help" program; rather, it is a spiritual program. Steps 1 and 2 put us in position to work the program. The program of action has God involved in it. After we make the decision in Step 3, we start using prayer. At Step 8 we have to have the willingness. If we don't have it, we pray for it until it comes.

Sometimes a sponsoree will have people on his list he feels have harmed him. Or for some other reason, he may feel strongly that he just doesn't want to make amends. He may have some all-or-nothing thinking, such as, *If I can't make amends to* all *the people on my list, I can't make amends to* any *of them. I can't take Step 9.*

I like to tell sponsorees, "Take a sheet of paper and make headings across from left to right: NOW—LATER—MAYBE—NEVER. List all the people you are willing to make amends to *right now.* Then list all you are willing to make amends to *a little later.* And people you *may* make amends to, but you're not sure." The sponsor should go over these lists with the sponsoree, and help her fill in the final column of people she is *never* going to make amends to. Often this list will include people toward whom she has deep-seated resentments.

In the process of making amends to the "easier" names on the list, the sponsoree most likely will find the results so satisfying that she will be motivated to go on! It's not as bad as she thought it would be. She will probably want to go on to the second column (the "later" column). She may want to go on even to the third list—often she will even become willing to do some of the ones on the *never* list. But she won't know until she gets started—and starts getting some results.

The key to Step 8 is to become willing. And there's also some timing to be considered here. Steps 8 and 9 are not like Steps 1 and 2, where all you must do is just realize something. Steps 8 and 9 are a process that takes time to complete—and some things may never be completed. The conditions the Step gives us for making amends "wherever possible," and "except when to do so would injure them or others" are likely to stretch the process out even longer. There may be people to whom we *can't* make amends because we do not know where they are or because they are dead. That's part of why Bill Wilson suggests that our freedom comes from our willingness.

Before you take the Step, you don't have any results. You only get the results from a Step after you take it.

You don't get results from talking about the Step.
You don't get results from reading about it.
You don't get results from intellectualizing about it.

You get the results from *doing* it.

The original step in the Oxford Groups was called "restitution." Bill Wilson no doubt felt that no self-respecting alcoholic would like this religious-sounding term. So he changed it to something he thought would be easier for alcoholics to apply. He divided it into two Steps, changing "restitution" to "made a list," then "became willing to make amends to the people on the list," then "made direct amends wherever possible."

Restitution seems to suggest repaying something material. The dictionary defines "restitution" as "the act of restoring a thing to its proper owner." But making amends means setting right a wrong in the broadest possible sense.

Restitution is necessarily a part of any spiritual program. But making amends is even more than restitution. So after we do Step 8, Bill says we "make direct amends." He starts describing "direct amends" in the middle of a paragraph on page 77:

The question of how to approach the man we hated will arise. It may be he has done us more harm than we have done him and, though we may have acquired a better attitude toward him, we are still not too keen about admitting our faults. Nevertheless, with a person we dislike, we take the bit in our teeth. It is harder to go to an enemy than to a friend, but we find it much more beneficial to us.

The sponsor should read this passage, continuing to the next page, with the sponsoree who is preparing to begin Step 9.

The Big Book says "we made direct amends . . . ," and the paragraph above tells us how to go to the "man we hated." This is an example of a face-to-face amend. We go into the man's office, face to face, and make a direct amend. This kind of amend is probably the most rewarding, because when you go to a person face to face and make an amend, you get the results immediately.

Bill Wilson also notes, "Most alcoholics owe money" (p. 78). So you might ask the sponsoree to categorize the amends:

- direct face-to-face amends, and
- money amends.

Often the money amends are easier, and so they can go on the "right now" list. This may mean making arrangements to pay a debt over time.

Most alcoholics, for their egos' sake, would like to get sacks full of money, go see the people they owe, drop a sack on their desks, and say, "Here's all the money I owe you." But we need the humility to approach these people we owe and to ask to make arrangements to repay it the best way we can. Usually we are worried about how we are going to be accepted, but most people we owe are going to be happy to get their money however they can. So we go to them, sit down, and work the payment out with them. Willingness is the key.

I might owe a person $2,000 about which I feel guilt, remorse, and even shame, but by using the Steps in this program, I can become willing to pay him, go see him, and give him $10 as the first payment on what I owe. When I walk out of his office, I will be free of the guilt, remorse, and shame!

We're not doing this simply to get over the debt, but to get over the emotional burden. If I can get him out of my head for $10, that's pretty cheap. Then I can pay on the debt until I finally get it paid off. Time will pass, and all these things will be straightened out. We can use the time, or we can waste it. If we're willing to do it, God will make it possible for us to do it, no matter what the sum is.

This takes courage. This is why we ask God in the Serenity Prayer for "the courage to change the things I can." We don't even expect to have enough courage; we must ask God for it!

For this reason Steps 8 and 9 sometimes are spread out over a lifetime. But if I'm willing, I am free from my fear and guilt and shame.

"Courage is mastery of fear—not absence of fear."

—Mark Twain

It's also important to consider that Step 9 says "wherever possible." "Wherever possible" is about both a time and a place. I've often heard people interpret this as "whenever possible." If you tell most alcoholics to do what they need to do "whenever possible," it may never get done!

But "wherever possible" is spiritual. When it comes

about, it will be the right time and the right place and the right situation for the person who is getting sober and the person he is making amends to. Only God knows this. But if you are willing to do it, the "wherever possible" will come about.

One day a friend was in my office when some people walked by the door. He said, "I'll be back in a minute." I could hear him talking to someone in the hall. When he came back, he said, "I have been owing that man amends for ten years. When I saw him walk by I knew it was the time and the place. So I made my amends." Sometimes "wherever possible" occurs in a flash like that.

Only God knows the attitude of that other person. Often as we have grown and gotten sober, as our lives have changed, and the attitude is right for both parties, God will make it possible for us to do what we have become willing to do.

As sponsors, we have a history of working with others on these Steps. We have found some people want to move too fast; others want to move too slowly. People don't like to make financial amends because they don't like to let go of their money—or they don't have any to let go of. And often they're paying for something they don't have anymore.

I've seen people have things like traffic fines they haven't paid. These are really amends to society that need to be paid. They're hard to pay, but usually the amount of money is not nearly as burdensome to us as the burden of fear we have, driving around worrying about getting stopped with fines unpaid! Or we may owe back taxes. Nobody enjoys paying taxes, but we have to make arrangements to do this, too, because we need the relief.

Even the courts will usually work with people. And there are ways to get credit straightened out. Businesses want you to have good credit so you can buy things, and they will usually help you return to the community. This may take some time. It is usually not an overnight matter. Some of these things we've been living with for years. I remember working with a guy who had twelve DWIs (driving-while-intoxicated charges). He made changes in his life. After he had been sober about six months, the judge, who had fined him $100,000, worked something out with him that he could deal with.

Many of the sexual harms your sponsoree may have been concerned with and had fears about will need to be categorized under " . . . except when to do so would injure them or others." If he keeps this in mind, he can't do anything about some of these. He will have to live with them.

I believe that as a sponsor, you should sit down and go over the Step 9 list with your sponsoree and advise him item by item on whether the need for amends should be acted on. The sponsoree needs guidance on these things. With financial harms, for example, it may be that the only way you can assess her ability to make amends is to know her income and obligations—in other words, her ability to make financial amends. You might draw up a budget with her. I've never seen an alcoholic who had a lot of financial discipline.

Step 9 may reveal many areas where the sponsoree needs guidance and assistance. He or she may have to make a lot of these decisions, but as the sponsor, you can help.

"Wherever possible" takes some people off our list; "when to do so would injure them or others" takes some people off. But we will put some of these back on as time changes situations and some previously impossible ones become possible. Chances are we will never get it all done. But our willingness, if it is genuine, will make us free.

The little pain we feel over the things that we are unable to make amends for is even good for us. It may make us treasure the relationships we have with other people and be more careful and considerate with them because of past experiences. It can make us better people.

> "We found that God does not make too hard terms for those who seek him."
>
> —*Alcoholics Anonymous,* p. 46

I have never sponsored a person who presented a problem that we couldn't find a solution to in the Big Book. Over the years, I have never worked with a person who wanted to get sober for whom I couldn't find workable answers in the Big Book. The Big Book covers every imaginable situation: financial problems, problems with the courts and the law, sexual infidelity, and anything else that might come up in specific sponsoring situations. You don't have to deal with these problems off the top of your head: you can go to the Big Book and learn how this specific problem is dealt with. And the sponsoree is more likely to feel confident about the suggested solutions to his problems if he feels they're coming directly from the program of recovery.

Guidance can be found in the Big Book . . .

Amends	Page(s)
Direct, face-to-face amends	77
Direct, owing money	78
For criminal offenses	78
Divorce, alimony, child support	79
Implicating others, getting permission	80
Domestic troubles	80–81
Extramarital sex, how much to tell	81

Jealousy	82
Cleaning house with the family	83
Wrongs we cannot right	83

Remember that we are "powerless," so the solution to our powerlessness is power. The main question we have to ask is, "How do we find power?" The purpose of the Book, of Steps 3 through 12, the plan of action, is to help us find power to solve our problems. It's very simple.

In Step 3 we made a decision to find the power. Steps 3 through 10 are designed to remove the things from ourselves that are blocking us from the power. With our minds full of guilt, remorse, and shame, God cannot direct our lives. Steps 4 through 10 remove these things from our minds and our lives so that Step 3 can be carried out. Only God can direct the life of an alcoholic or addict who has been living by self-will, whose life has been run by his reaction to other people and to things.

The Steps help us put our lives in order:

- We make a decision in Step 3 (as the result of Steps 1 and 2) that God will direct our lives. That corrects the center of our lives.
- We work on the mind in Steps 4, 5, 6, and 7. Things in the mind had God blocked in. With self at the center, we had developed habits of mind that allowed others to direct our lives (through our resentments, fears, and so on). Steps 4, 5, 6, and 7 clear our minds so that God can direct us.
- We clear up our relationships with others in Steps 8 and 9. We do this by acknowledging our wrongdoing and, wherever possible, making appropriate restitution.
- Now our lives are in order. We can use them as God intended.

In a successful life, God will be the director; the mind will be clear of emotional problems and will function with all its ability. Before God directed our lives, we directed them. We were living to satisfy the basic instincts, to satisfy self. We were using God for a troubleshooter and other people for our own desires. This is a complete change—living our lives as they were designed to be lived. When we use our lives as they were designed to be used, we have happiness, serenity, contentment.

———

The sponsoree undertakes Step 9 to change his character, not to change the immediate conditions of his life. You know, sometimes we are motivated to do these difficult, dangerous things not so much because we have guts, but because we are desperate to change. If your sponsoree thinks about it, that not long ago he was struggling to take Step 1, and now he has the courage to take on Step 9, he should realize that he has had a lot of growth in his life already.

I often hear people say that after Step 9 come "the promises," but I prefer the term "results." I think Bill means these are the results of our work:

> We are going to know a new freedom and a new happiness. We will not regret the past nor wish to shut the door on it. We will comprehend the word serenity and we will know peace. No matter how far down the scale we have gone, we will see how our experience can benefit others. That feeling of uselessness and self-pity will disappear. We will lose interest in selfish things and gain interest in our fellows. Self-seeking will slip away. Our whole attitude and outlook on life will change. Fear of people and of economic insecurity will leave us. We will intuitively know how to handle situations that used to baffle us. We will suddenly realize that God is doing for us what we could not do for ourselves. (pp. 83–84)

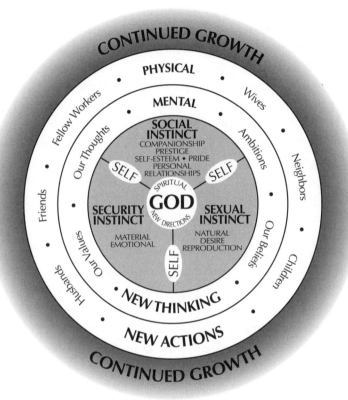

In Step 1 we grasp the problem. In Step 2 we see the solution, but there are not really any results there. These can be compared to the doctor diagnosing a problem. By diagnosing it, she hasn't made you feel any better. It's just put her in a position to write the prescription. Even the prescription doesn't make you well. You have to get the prescription filled, go home and take your medicine, and over a period of days, as a result of actually taking the medicine, you begin to recover. You get well based on the actions you take, not on Step 1 and Step 2.

So the action Steps all have directions, actions, and results. You improve as you take the actions. You know, the worst problem in medicine is that patients don't follow through. The doctor diagnoses the problem, prescribes a program of recovery, but the patient doesn't follow the program of action that the doctor has prescribed. It is the same with this program. Once we have identified the problem and found the solution, we don't get results until we take the actions that are required.

The therapeutic Steps are action Steps, Steps 4, 5, 6, 7, 8, and 9. All these are actions we had to take to carry out the decision in Step 3. Each of these Steps produced a change, finally culminating in a personality change sufficient to recover at Step 9. This process is called the "spiritual awakening" or the "spiritual experience."

Are these extravagant promises? They are being fulfilled among us—

| sometimes quickly | . . . a spiritual experience |
| sometimes slowly | . . . a spiritual awakening |

They will always materialize if we work for them.

—Adapted from *Alcoholics Anonymous*, p. 84

Bill Wilson admonishes us to pray: "Reminding ourselves that we had decided to go to any lengths to find a spiritual experience, we asked that we be given strength and direction to do the right thing no matter what the personal consequences" (p. 79).

You may see "revolutionary changes" in your sponsoree —a complete turnaround:

- personality changes sufficient to recover
- religious experience
- sudden and spectacular upheaval
- sudden revolutionary changes
- immediate and overwhelming God-consciousness
- vast change in feeling and outlook
- transformations
- profound alterations

(adapted from *Alcoholics Anonymous*, p. 569)

All these phrases mean one thing—change!

And we come to realize their value, because these changes are "the beginning of the end of isolation from our fellows and from God" (*Twelve Steps and Twelve Traditions*, p. 82).

ASSIGNMENT FOR STEPS 10, 11, AND 12

READING . . . FOR SPONSOREE

Ask your sponsoree to read chapter 6, pages 84–88, and all of Chapter 7.

DISCUSSION . . . FOR SPONSOR

The last three Steps are more or less self-taught. They are a natural continuation of the process. Prayer and meditation become a natural part of a person's make-up. And wanting to tell other people is a natural extension of the process.

Continuing to Grow

I was to test my thinking by my new God-consciousness within. Common sense would thus become uncommon sense. I was to sit quietly when in doubt, asking only for direction and strength to meet my problems as He would have me.

—Bill W.,
Alcoholics Anonymous

STEP 10:
Continued to take personal inventory and when we were wrong promptly admitted it.

STEP 11:
Sought through prayer and meditation to improve our conscious contact with God as we understood Him, praying only for knowledge of His will for us and the power to carry that out.

STEP 12:
Having had a spiritual awakening as the result of these Steps, we tried to carry this message to alcoholics, and to practice these principles in all our affairs.

We learn by listening, we learn by example, and we learn by experience. And we learn by showing someone else. That's what Steps 10, 11, and 12 are all about.

Step 10 is not a new Step. In a way, it's a summary of all the Steps that have come before. Step 10 is how we continue to grow. It's a way to live. If we want to remain sober, we have to continue to grow. We can't just maintain. Even though Step 11 says we have a "daily reprieve contingent on the maintenance of our spiritual condition" (p. 85), we must not take this to mean a static, unchanging situation. Although you sometimes hear them referred to as "maintenance" Steps, this is not maintenance seen as holding steady once and for all at some place we've reached. It is maintaining through growing.

Maintaining our spiritual condition *requires growth.* Everything in nature either grows or withers. If we don't continue to grow spiritually in our sobriety, we are going to get worse.

When a person starts working Step 10, he learns more. I think this is when he should start sponsoring other people. He is now familiar with using the Steps, and he is fresh. He can become a good sponsor.

Most people who don't sponsor in their first year of sobriety never sponsor. I think sponsorship should begin when we are fresh off the Steps and have a new experience to share; if we wait around, we may forget how we accomplished it. When your sponsoree gets to Step 10, he or she should probably start sponsoring.

We don't get any growth following Step 1—no therapeutic value, no improvement. We don't get any growth after Step 2. And, even though everybody expects a lot, we don't really even get any after Step 3. All the personality changes begin after the action Steps.

Step 4 is the first Step that gives us a change. Step 5 gives us a personality change. So do 6 and 7, 8 and 9. Step 10 is a daily practicing of all the changing Steps.

As we re-practice these action Steps through Step 10

over and over, we will continue to grow. The more often we take Steps 4 and 5 in doing Step 10, the more we learn about them and the better we become. As we ask God to remove the character defects in 6 and 7, these defects become fewer and fewer. And as we make amends for the harms we have done to other people, our relationships with other people improve. So we see how the continuous working of these Steps will keep us free of the things that block us from God. We will maintain our sobriety—and our lives will continue to improve.

Once we have practiced Steps 1 through 9, we have the skills to develop a "personal inventory." The word *personal* in Step 10 suggests that it is more than the inventory we took of our thought processes in Step 4. It's a broader inventory that examines the life we live each day. And personal means private and unique to the individual—one that fits each personality. In a good personal inventory, the individual can see his relationship with himself, with God, and with everyone and everything he interacts with. He can learn more about himself each day. He can gain a unique understanding of where problems may occur. He has his own unique patterns to look for. The more he learns about himself, the better he can interact with the world, with everything around him— his family, his job, his friends, other people.

Throughout the Big Book, Bill Wilson discusses the three dimensions of life:

- The spiritual, our very core.
- The mental, the life of the mind.
- The physical and social, the most visible part of our lives.

If we think of our lives as made up of these three concentric circles, most people focus first on the outer circle— their actions and their relationships with other people—

because this part is visible. This outer circle is made up of our jobs, our money, our health, our homes and families—everything we interact with. Most people think, *If I had this all together, I would be happy inside.* But that would be working from the outside in. And we know that *everything in nature grows from the inside out.* This is not a new principle. It's the principle of life contained in the books of every great religion. A.A. didn't design this—it is a principle of life.

When we come into the program, our lives are not God-centered, they are self-centered. So we have self—rather than God—at the core of our lives, and having self at our core messes up our thinking and our relationships with other people. The principles of the program are about putting our lives back together and in proper order. That's what we've been doing with these first nine simple Steps.

Teach us to order our days rightly,

That we may enter the gate of wisdom.

—Psalm 90:12, *The New American Bible*

This is the miracle of A.A.: you can take something as complicated as a human life misused, and with nine simple Steps put it all back together the way it was meant to be. The Big Book discusses a design for living that works!

Now having worked the Steps, having put our lives in order, we are ready to grow. Through the application of these principles, we can grow into another dimension of living, where we will "know happiness, peace, and usefulness, in a way of life that is incredibly more wonderful as time passes" (p. 8). Bill Wilson called it "the fourth dimension" (p. 8).

People who have lost their old lives have to learn to live

Three Dimensions of Life: Steps 1 through 9

There are three dimensions of life:

Spiritual	Steps 1 • 2 • 3
Mental	Steps 4 • 5 • 6 • 7
Physical • Social	Steps 8 • 9

a new way. It's an advantage of recovery that we can live better than most other people because we have been forced to find a principled way to live. We have to in order to recover. I often think that if recovering people were forced to live the lives most people classify as "normal," they would have to use or drink, because what some call "normal" often looks pretty sick. We have to live better than normal people.

But living in the fourth dimension takes work. The more we practice the tenth Step, the more we learn about ourselves, the more we grow to another level. What happens when we grow to another level? Once we grow into another level, things we have stubbornly held onto may become objectionable, and we will want to get rid of them. We'll have more things come to the surface that we want to get rid of, and we will keep growing. This will come about as we work with new people and continue to work our program. Growth is a natural and exciting part of our lives.

———

The tenth Step is one of the greatest growth Steps in the whole program. If you ask a person who has been in the program a long time, she will likely tell you that most of the growth of her life has come through using the tenth Step.

When you grow in the first three dimensions, your thinking is naturally going to rise to a much higher plane. The Big Book tells us of many things we will be able to do as the result of working the Steps. We are told that our old ideas will be cast aside and new ideas will dominate. The third dimension that we have been most interested in—our relationships, our health, our financial situations—all these things will have improved. These things are beyond our imagination when we are still drinking or using drugs, when our lives are still in shambles.

Daily Inventory

When we retire at night, we constructively review our day.
Were we resentful, selfish, dishonest, or afraid?

PERSONALITY CHARACTERISTICS OF SELF-WILL	PERSONALITY CHARACTERISTICS OF GOD'S WILL
Selfishness and Self-seeking	Interest in Others
Dishonesty	Honesty
Fear	Courage
Inconsideration	Consideration
Pride	Humility—Seeking God's Will
Greed	Giving or Sharing
Lust	Doing For Others
Anger	Calmness
Envy	Gratitude
Sloth	Taking Action
Gluttony	Moderation
Impatience	Patience
Intolerance	Tolerance
Resentment	Forgiveness
Hate	Love—Concern for Others
Harmful Acts	Good Deeds
Self-pity	Self-forgetfulness
Self-justification	Humility—Seeking God's Will
Self-importance	Modesty
Self-condemnation	Self-forgiveness
Suspicion	Trust
Doubt	Faith

What we really have is a daily reprieve contingent on the maintenance of our spiritual condition. Every day is a day when we must carry the vision of God's will into all our activities.

—*Alcoholics Anonymous,* p. 85

Most of us have been pretty aware of our third dimension, even if it has been totally destroyed sometimes. Most alcoholics will tell you that straightening up these third-dimension things takes so much of their time that they don't have time to work on the fourth dimension. But you can rest assured that you can't do anything about the third dimension—the outer world—until you have done something about the first dimension, your inner core.

You can't really concentrate on the fourth dimension; you simply work on the first three dimensions—spiritual, mental, physical—and as you grow, you'll automatically grow into the fourth dimension.

When I came to A.A., my marriage was on the rocks. I didn't have a job. I didn't have any money. I was pretty well shot. My sponsor told me, "You have to get your life straightened out."

I said, "I know; I gotta go to work."

He said, "Do you work?"

I figured he must think I was some kind of bum. I said, "Sure I work. I've been working since I was eleven years old!"

He asked me, "What do you have to go to work for?"

I said, "I don't have any money!"

He said, "If you've been working since you were eleven years old and still don't have any money, you aren't doing much good working. You ought to try something else. Maybe you should try getting sober first."

This kind of outer problem is all we can see at this stage.

But when you see a person who has a good spiritual program, he can take care of his money and the other things in his life. In Step 10, we're putting the three dimensions in our life together.

Most sponsors will be able to help people because they have had to put their own lives back together. We know it takes some doing. For the newly sober person, it means facing her financial situation, her obligations, making amends—in short, working the Steps. But regardless of how complicated and difficult it may seem when she begins, she will look back on it one day and be proud of what she has accomplished. The sponsor should be there while she is going through this—sometimes to slow her down, sometimes to speed her up.

Sometimes you may not know exactly what advice to give someone you are working with. At those times you have other people in the program *you* can talk to. You might occasionally need to tell a sponsoree, "Let me talk to you some more tomorrow night about this before you do anything." Then you can talk to friends in the program, get the benefit of their experience, and then get back to the sponsoree.

You might even feel it is appropriate sometimes to send the sponsoree to that other person to talk to him or her directly. We can use the expertise of all our people. I often send sponsorees to talk to people I know in the program who have more financial expertise than I do. We all help each other. Whatever the problem, someone within our fellowship has helpful information and insights.

Worksheet talks are good too. (See box.) But you need to do them right. I've seen sponsors give worksheets to brand new people. After a person has worked the first five Steps, he can benefit from hearing how some other people have worked the Steps, but I don't think worksheets are as useful when they are given to brand new people.

USING WORKSHEETS. . .

In the early days of A.A., people were looking for ways to work with other alcoholics. After a person had been in the program for a period of time, he was given a worksheet with the names and phone numbers of a number of people in recovery. The new prospect was advised to call these people and set up an appointment to visit. He was to ask these people to describe to him how they had worked the Steps. These visits were very helpful, and they became an integral part of sponsorship in many places.

I always feel honored when someone puts me on a worksheet. When someone comes to me and tells me his sponsor has put my name on his worksheet, I usually ask him whether he has completed Step 5. If he has, I make a special time to talk to him. If he says he hasn't, I suggest that he come back when he's completed Step 5—because until he does, he doesn't really have the foundation he needs.

You can't just give somebody a worksheet list and *hope* it's going to have some kind of magical effect. The same thing is true of the stories in the back of the Big Book. If you are working the Steps, the stories are helpful, but if you haven't worked your Steps, they have no real value. A lot of people hope they can go to meetings and read the stories in the back of the Big Book instead of going to the trouble to work the Steps.

The worksheet is a useful tool when it's done right. A sponsor makes a list of people in the fellowship willing to talk to new people and tell them about their own sobriety. He instructs his sponsoree to contact the people on the list and make an appointment to talk to them for a few minutes.

When we are making a worksheet list, sometimes we can send a sponsoree with financial problems to somebody we know has some expertise, but as a general rule we can't really match people up. Remember this is a spiritual program. I think we do well just to send our sponsorees to talk to people who we feel have worked the Steps and who have a good program.

One of the therapeutic things that often happens is that the new person goes to talk to a busy person and sees that the person is willing to take time out of his schedule to talk. I think this usually impresses the new person.

It also has a good effect from the point of view of the social needs of the third dimension, to see that these sober, straight people, these good models, are welcoming them into the fellowship, that they are willing to share their experience, strength, and hope. Every time the sponsor hands out a worksheet, he or she is doing something that rebinds the fellowship. This is an experience a sponsoree will always remember.

Once we have worked Step 10, the Book gives us more promises:

> We have ceased fighting anything or anyone—even alcohol. By this time sanity will have returned. We will seldom be interested in liquor. If tempted, we recoil from it as from a hot flame. We react sanely and normally. We will see that this has happened automatically. We will see that our new attitude toward liquor has been given us without any thought or effort on our part. It just comes! We are not fighting it, neither are we avoiding temptation. We feel as though we had been placed in a position of neutrality—safe and protected. We have not even sworn off. The problem has been removed. It does not exist for us. We are neither cocky nor are we afraid. That is how we react so long as we keep in fit spiritual condition. (pp. 84–85)

Worksheet Talks

	1.	2. SUMMARY	3. CD/I*
1.	DATE ASSIGNED		
	NAME		
	TELEPHONE		
2.	DATE ASSIGNED		
	NAME		
	TELEPHONE		
3.	DATE ASSIGNED		
	NAME		
	TELEPHONE		
4.	DATE ASSIGNED		
	NAME		
	TELEPHONE		

5.	DATE ASSIGNED			
	NAME			
	TELEPHONE			
6.	DATE ASSIGNED			
	NAME			
	TELEPHONE			
7.	DATE ASSIGNED			
	NAME			
	TELEPHONE			
8.	DATE ASSIGNED			
	NAME			
	TELEPHONE			

*Completion date and initials of counselor or sponsor

As we grow from the center of ourselves out, we push ourselves or expand outward into the fourth dimension. The fourth dimension is unlimited, unbounded.

Ours is a spiritual program.
This means that while we don't have all the answers,
we have access to a Power that does.

The sponsoree should look at how his work life and his financial life have changed since he worked the Steps. He can look at what's in the third dimension: everything physical and social, the world he lives in, and his actions, what he does every day. Many people think that if they can get these things straightened out, they will be happy. But, you know, we can't fix these exterior things at all. We make ourselves, our inner core, right, and then the elements of the third dimension, the material and social world, become right. Jesus taught us: "Seek ye first the Kingdom of God and all these things will be added to you" (Matthew 6:33).

If you study the basics of all the great religions—never mind the doctrines—they all say the same thing in one way or another. This is the way life is supposed to work.

The Steps put our lives back in order. They are a set of directions for living our lives. When you use a thing as it was designed to be used, it works. Through the Steps, we take a messed-up life and put it all back together again, Step by Step. I don't care what the problem is—if we get our lives together, the problems will take care of themselves. Now we see that the program is all about living instead of just about not drinking.

This understanding has informed my life. This is the principle, the design, of life.

We don't always get this across to people: since your life has a design, you have to use it as it was designed! Sometimes I've set a hinge in a door and door frame. If you are like me, you don't usually have a sharp wood chisel. So you go into your toolbox, and since you don't have a wood chisel, you try to do it with your screwdriver. Well, a screwdriver was designed to install and take out screws, and it usually does an efficient job of this work. But if you hammer on it trying to use it to cut out hinge notches in your door frame, it won't work very well for that—and later, when you try to use it to put in or take out screws, it won't work very well for that anymore either. You didn't use it as it was designed to be used.

We do the same thing with our lives. The misuse manifests itself in drug and alcohol abuse and other things. We can use these Steps, the principles of living, to put our lives back in order.

It's a miracle that we can do this by applying the principles in nine simple Steps. We can put our lives back in order! We want it to be more complicated because when we have our lives so fouled up, it seems more complicated.

When you create something, you are the one most able to write the directions on how to use it. The manufacturers of products and gadgets usually warn purchasers that if they don't follow the directions, the guarantee is not any good. God created human beings and He gave us a set of directions to tell us how a human life is supposed to work. The Bible, the Big Book, the texts of every great religion have these directions. As these religions have grown, though, often they have become discouraged about teaching the principles of how it's supposed to work; perhaps they feel they don't have time. So they just hang the rules on the wall telling people what *not* to do. But they often don't tell them how not to do it. We always break the rules if we don't understand the principles. But we find that if we understand the principles, we don't need the rules in the same way.

In A.A. we teach principles. Principles don't change; they are lasting. But teaching and learning principles takes time and it takes work. Rules don't work well with alcoholics. Most alcoholics see rules as a challenge. They try to figure how to get around them, how to find exceptions! So we offer principles. Sometimes, though, even in A.A., we have sponsors who try to make rules instead of going to the trouble to teach principles.

We need to keep teaching people the principles of living. You know, our prisons are full because people can't figure out how to live. Federal, state, county, city lawmakers —all of them are constantly writing laws, and our prisons are still full because people can't figure out how to live. Nobody is trying to teach people how to live, but we spend millions working on the third dimension—trying to control each other's behavior.

Our living experiences are the result of the thoughts we produce today. Our thoughts are governed either by us or by God—by our will or by God's will. Our basic instincts produce our thinking, and our thinking produces our actions, and that determines how we live our lives.

"Let one therefore keep the mind pure,
for what a person thinks, that he becomes."

—the *Upanishads*

Human law does not govern the spiritual part of us or the mental part of us. A person in prison is there because of actions he took. A person doesn't go to prison for what he thinks; he goes to prison for what he does.

As a society we put the person in prison to punish his actions, but we don't change his thinking. When we release him from prison, he still has the same thinking—maybe even worse from having been there. He usually gets out and becomes a "repeat offender." That person won't stay out of prison until he changes his actions. But in truth, the only way he can change his actions is to change the way he thinks, through his spiritual life.

———

When you learn the principles in one program for living, like A.A., you can see them in all the others. They may seem different on the surface, but inside they are basically the same.

> Some people think that A.A. came from the Bible, but I think it's more likely A.A. came from the same place the Bible came from.

If the sponsoree has effectively worked the first nine Steps, he has some ideas about prayer and meditation. These have to be polished and refined, but it's a kind of natural process. You can ask him to go over Step 11 in the Big Book (see page 86). This is one of the clearest and best-developed discussions of any Step. Bill Wilson was understandably reluctant to write about prayer and meditation because at that time he didn't believe he had any real depth of understanding about prayer and meditation. He doesn't try to teach us how to pray and meditate. Neither can we teach another person how to pray and meditate without the danger of teaching him *our* concept. In the process, we might even destroy his individual concept. So we shy away from doing that.

What you *can do* as a sponsor is give what Bill Wilson calls "definite and valuable suggestions" (p. 86). You can identify them for your sponsoree. If he or she follows them, it's likely that prayer and meditation will come naturally. The sponsor doesn't try to teach the sponsoree how to pray and meditate. The sponsoree will use these suggestions to teach himself.

One of the things I like about these suggestions is that they can be associated with certain normal activities in our lives. For example, it is suggested that "when we retire at night," something we do every day, we review our day. The therapeutic value of this is in seeing the good you did in the day—or in seeing what you could have done better. We humans do make mistakes. If we can learn the lessons from these mistakes, we are less likely to repeat them. In this way we can look at mistakes as positive things because overcoming them can make our lives better if we see the lessons in them. We should be willing to learn the lessons of a day in the day—and move on.

Human beings make mistakes.

We don't berate ourselves for our mistakes—we learn from them.

The next suggestion is about what we do when we get up in the morning: we ask God to direct our thinking. Once again, this is a daily activity that should become a habit.

The next suggestion deals with indecision. Way back when we did Step 3, we asked God to direct our lives. At Step 11, now that we have worked the program of action and cleared out the things that had blocked us from God, we are about to receive God's direction.

At times we may face indecision; we may not know which direction to take. So we stop; we take it easy. We don't struggle. We turn it over to God. The right answer will come.

We have all had hunches or inspiration, but now, using this technique, our "hunches" can gradually become a working part of our minds. This is difficult to learn at first, but after a while it becomes easier. Sometimes we have to say, "I don't know." Then we relax and turn it over to God. The Big Book says if we can make this a working part of our minds, we can turn to it whenever we need to, whenever we are faced with indecision (p. 86).

You can help your sponsoree see it: there isn't a problem in the world that you can't get an answer to. You can help your sponsoree see that he is on pretty firm ground.

The next suggestion is how we should pray. It's very broad, something anybody can learn to do. He reminds us that we pray *only* for the knowledge of His will for us and the power to carry that out. If we carry out God's will, we are following God's way of life.

Bill Wilson offers some "definite and valuable suggestions" on prayer and meditation . . .

Night:	We constructively review our day.
Morning:	We ask God to direct our thoughts.
Indecision:	We relax and take it easy; we ask God for inspiration.

We pray "that we be shown all through the day what our next step is to be, that we be given whatever we need to take care of such problems. We ask especially for freedom from self-will, and are careful to make no request for ourselves only . . ." —*Alcoholics Anonymous*, p. 87

You know, we don't have to pray for material things. We pray for God's will. If we carry out God's will, our material needs will be met. Jesus taught us in the Lord's Prayer to ask, "Give us this day our daily bread." *Bread* means all of our needs for that day. We're not given enough for a week; we're given enough for one day. And we tend to overload the day with problems of yesterday and of tomorrow. This puts a strain on the bread for that day! Our part is to keep our focus on only one day; God will supply our needs for that day.

Every one of us was put here on Earth to serve a specific purpose, to do a specific "job"; that is God's will for us. We have within us the knowledge of what that job is. The challenge is whether we do that job while we are here, or whether we go do our own thing. I've learned from many years of experience that the happiest we will ever be is when we can find out what our job is and start doing it. We will feel better, perform better, be better, because we will be in God's purpose.

"THROUGH PRAYER AND MEDITATION . . ."

Recently at a Big Book Study, someone said that the human mind gathers all the data in a process: our eyes send a picture to our brain; our ears, our nose, our sense of touch, all these report to the brain; and the brain analyzes these messages and reacts to them. But, he said, we also have another sense. People usually associate "listening" only with what we hear with our ears, but he suggested that meditation is another sense, another way of listening. We can become able to listen to this sense and act on the data it sends us even when its message seems contrary to the information we're getting from our other senses.

Each chapter in this book about a Step has opened with an excerpt from Bill Wilson's description of his first experience with what was to become the Twelve Steps. This chapter's headnote was Bill's description of his own Step 12. That passage states the essence of the program:

> I was to test my thinking by my new God-consciousness within. Common sense would thus become uncommon sense. I was to sit quietly when in doubt, asking only for direction and strength to meet my problems as He would have me. Never was I to pray for myself, except as my requests bore on my usefulness to others. Then only might I expect to receive. But that would be in great measure.
>
> My friend [Ebby] promised when these things were done I would enter upon a new relationship with my Creator; that I would have the elements of a way of living which answered all my problems. Belief in the power of God, plus enough willingness, honesty, and humility to establish and maintain the new order of things, were the essential requirements.
>
> (*Alcoholics Anonymous*,
> pp. 13–14)

We are fortunate to carry *this* message.

The Word from Joe

'It's gonna be okay'

Friday, November 2, 2007

LITTLE ROCK — LIFE IS STRANGE. That's not an original observation, since life keeps demonstrating just how strange it is. Consider the life and saving times of Joseph Daniel McQuany, 1928-2007. Mr. McQuany, who became much better known as just Joe around Little Rock, was one of the most successful people we've ever heard of.

Joe touched, indeed transformed, the lives of who knows how many tens of thousands in his city, state, country and beyond. He started an enterprise on a shoestring or less-a $330 grant and some charitable donations-that grew into a publishing company, traveling mission, growing institution, and, most important, a blessing.

The secret of his success? "If I hadn't been an alcoholic," he confided to one of the many groups he addressed, "I probably would have amounted to nothing."

And all because one day back in 1962, Joe McQuany decided he'd get sober. In those days, he'd recall, white men trying to get on the wagon could find a treatment program, black men were sent to the State Hospital-aka the Nut House in the patois of the times-and as for women alcoholics, the only place for them was jail.

Once detoxed, Joe McQuany knew he'd have to find some way to stay sober. His way was Alcoholics Anonymous, even though, in 1962, as a black man he would be left out of the social bonding that's such an important if informal part of its program. No matter. He had the Twelve Steps, AA's version of the Ten Commandments, and the Big Book. A testament and a faith. What more does a natural leader need? Build on it and the people will come.

Soon the man was organizing AA groups himself. He was a whiz at it. Not only because he'd been there and knew the cravings and excuses, the real desperation and false exhilaration of it all, but maybe because to save himself he had to save others.

JOE McQUANY wound up founding an offshoot of AA himself. He called his program Serenity House before it had a house-an old one on Broadway in Little Rock. As his program grew, he moved it to larger and larger quarters.

Serenity House became Serenity Park-an extended-care sanctuary for all, black or white, penniless or professional, who needed to get that monkey off their back. You might be surprised at the nice, outwardly successful people who are chemically dependent slaves. Then again, if you've had much experience of the world, you probably wouldn't be.

Mainly people came to Serenity House not because of the books Joe McQuany would write, or lectures he would give, or the programs he devised, but because of Joe himself. To quote one of his coworkers and admirers-but we repeat ourselves-his soft, unjudging brown eyes would connect with the souls of others. Joe seemed to look past all the superficialities that separate us from one another and see within the whole creature, sinner man.

You may have met people like Joe on rare occasion-if you've been fortunate. They've got something special about them, a kind of almost palpable aura. And you never forget them. They're always there for you; they're always there for everybody. The short word for them may be saints.

The man never tired, not even during his last, four-year struggle with Parkinson's, and he never stopped dreaming. His last great dream was a treatment center for women. When the ground was broken for that project two years ago, and folks asked where the money was coming from to finish it, Joe told the paper: "I had $300 [when I started]. People said, 'How are you gonna do it?' I said, 'I don't know,' and I stepped out. I've always stepped out into things, and people have always helped me."

They did again. Construction was completed a few weeks ago, and Joe was there to admire the finished work. It was another of his dreams achieved.

He didn't seem surprised. Sitting on a patio overlooking the new building just days before he went into the hospital for the last time, Joe McQuany kicked back and observed, "It's gonna be okay." JOE McQUANY could have been talking about a lot more than a building; he could have been summing up the message he'd brought to so many, whatever their station in life, who were poor in spirit. Then they would read one of his books, or leave one of his lectures renewed and resolved, or check out of Serenity House rich in hope and determination. That might've been all they had, but they knew it was going to be enough, it was gonna be okay. A short word for that attitude is faith.

Joe taught folks faith, or rather he would let them come to it. Much as someone might point out the quality of the light on a beautiful fall day, or a harvest moon shining above, or the grace all around us. When it came to knowing how to live a full life free and unhindered, Joe McQuany was his own best example.

At his death last week, condolences poured in from all over, including nearly every state in the Union and 10 foreign countries at last count. His obituary noted that Joseph Daniel McQuany left behind his wife of 48 years, Loubelle, numerous family (including 12 greatgrandchildren), and "friends around the world." Many of those friends have the best of reasons to be grateful for Joe: a life of their own-rather than one dictated by the current addiction.

Joe always lived simply. He was interested in a richer life: helping others. Reading this today may be someone out there who is heavy-burdened, convinced that if it weren't for the particular chemical cross he has to bear, he'd live fully, do great things, amount to something. In 1962 Joe McQuany found himself in that spot, desperate over his weakness, and proceeded to . . . turn it into a strength. So can you, Troubled Reader. "If I hadn't been an alcoholic, I probably would have amounted to nothing."

Editorial used with permission, ©2007, Arkansas Democrat-Gazette

11/02/2007

References

Alcoholics Anonymous, 3rd edition, New York: Alcoholics Anonymous World Services, Inc., 1976. (The "Big Book")

Alcoholics Anonymous Comes of Age: A Brief History of A.A., New York: Alcoholics Anonymous Publishing, Inc., 1957.

Twelve Steps and Twelve Traditions, New York: Alcoholics Anonymous World Services, Inc, 1981. (The "Twelve and Twelve")

Mel B., *New Wine,* Center City, Minnesota: Hazelden Foundation, 1991.

ADDRESSES

Alcoholics Anonymous World Services, Inc.
P.O. Box 459
Grand Central Station
New York, New York 10163
www.alcoholics-anonymous.org

Al-Anon WSO
1600 Corporate Landing
Virginia Beach, VA 23454
www.al-anon-alateen.org

Kelly Foundation
2801 West Roosevelt Road
Little Rock, AR 72204
www.kellyfdn.com